Lunar JUMBLE®

A Total Eclipse of Puzzles!

Henri Arnold,
Bob Lee,
Mike Argirion,
Jeff Knurek, and
David L. Hoyt

TRIUMPH
BOOKS

Jumble® is a registered trademark
of Tribune Media Services, Inc.

Copyright © 2013 by Tribune Media Services, Inc.
All rights reserved.

This book is available in quantity at special discounts
for your group or organization.

For further information, contact:

Triumph Books LLC
814 North Franklin Street
Chicago, Illinois 60610
Phone: (312) 337-0747
www.triumphbooks.com

Printed in U.S.A.

ISBN: 978-1-60078-853-6

Design by Sue Knopf

CONTENTS

Lunar JUMBLE®

Classic Puzzles

JUMBLE®

Unscramble these four Jumbles, one letter to each square, to form four ordinary words.

UPYTT

NALAC

PECDIT

ARXOTH

WHAT THE MANICURIST'S CUSTOMER WAS GETTING.

Now arrange the circled letters to form the surprise answer, as suggested by the above cartoon.

Print answer here ☐☐☐ OF ☐☐☐☐

JUMBLE®

Unscramble these six Jumbles, one letter to each square, to form six ordinary words.

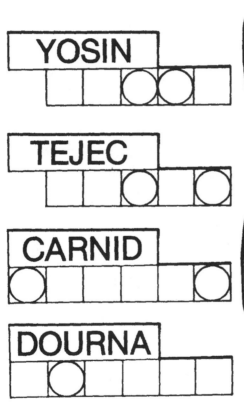

YOSIN

TEJEC

CARNID

DOURNA

Trouble is we spoiled him

WHAT THE LOAFER WHO WAS BORN WITH A SILVER SPOON IN HIS MOUTH HASN'T DONE SINCE.

Now arrange the circled letters to form the surprise answer, as suggested by the above cartoon.

Print answer here

JUMBLE®

Unscramble these four Jumbles, one letter to
each square, to form four ordinary words.

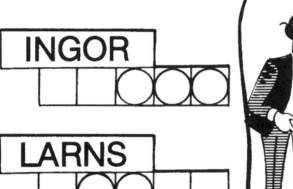

INGOR

LARNS

SAURES

GLOUEY

THIS SHOULD ONLY
BE DONE WITH
GOOD TASTE.

Now arrange the circled letters to form
the surprise answer, as suggested by the
above cartoon.

Print answer here

4

JUMBLE®

Unscramble these four Jumbles, one letter to each square, to form four ordinary words.

SYSEM

THYFE

GITHEY

PENMAD

Agreed?   ¡Agreed!

YOU MIGHT SEE
EYE TO EYE
WITH SOMEONE
WHO'S THIS.

Now arrange the circled letters to form the surprise answer, as suggested by the above cartoon.

Print answer here   THE ☐☐☐☐☐ ☐☐☐☐☐☐

5

JUMBLE®

Unscramble these four Jumbles, one letter to each square, to form four ordinary words.

TIFUR

RETEX

SOWDRY

CURPSE

Chocolate?

I'm on a diet

INSTEAD OF ICE CREAM, EPICURES MIGHT "GO FOR" THIS.

Now arrange the circled letters to form the surprise answer, as suggested by the above cartoon.

Print answer here " ◯◯◯◯ ◯◯◯◯ "

JUMBLE®

Unscramble these four Jumbles, one letter to each square, to form four ordinary words.

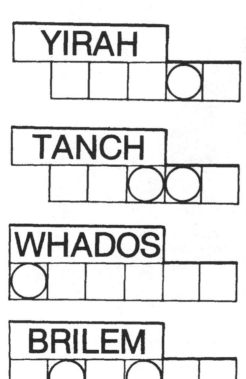

YIRAH

TANCH

WHADOS

BRILEM

He's real sharp!

SOMETHING YOU'RE SURE TO FIND IN AN ALGEBRA INSTRUCTOR, IF HE'S AS SMART AS HE SHOULD BE.

Now arrange the circled letters to form the surprise answer, as suggested by the above cartoon.

Print answer here

JUMBLE®

Unscramble these four Jumbles, one letter to
each square, to form four ordinary words.

TYSUL

FINKE

INSPOO

UNTTAR

Welcome to my house. How about joining our little card game?

HE MIGHT SEEM HOSPITABLE, BUT NOT TO BE TRUSTED WHEN HE DOES THIS.

Now arrange the circled letters to form
the surprise answer, as suggested by the
above cartoon.

Print answer here " ❍❍❍❍❍   ❍❍❍   ❍❍ "

JUMBLE®

Unscramble these four Jumbles, one letter to each square, to form four ordinary words.

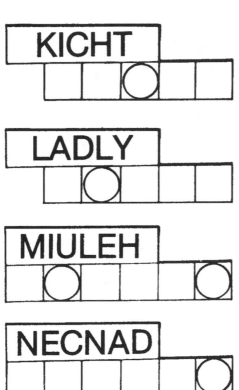

KICHT

LADLY

MIULEH

NECNAD

But let me make one thing perfectly clear...

"AIMED" TO PROVIDE CHANNELS FOR COMMUNICATION.

Now arrange the circled letters to form the surprise answer, as suggested by the above cartoon.

Print answer here  " ⬡⬡⬡⬡⬡ "

JUMBLE®

Unscramble these four Jumbles, one letter to each square, to form four ordinary words.

CROAG

GOLIC

FORLEG

THEVIR

WHAT THE PAS— SENGERS GOT WHEN THE AIR CONDITION— ING FAILED.

Now arrange the circled letters to form the surprise answer, as suggested by the above cartoon.

Print answer here ☐☐☐ UNDER THE ☐☐☐☐☐☐

JUMBLE®

Unscramble these four Jumbles, one letter to each square, to form four ordinary words.

CHULG

CRAFS

REWEPT

LENKER

A lucky break—for him

BY A STROKE OF LUCK, THIS FISH GOT AWAY— OR SO IT SOUNDS.

Now arrange the circled letters to form the surprise answer, as suggested by the above cartoon.

Print answer here ◯ " ◯◯◯◯◯ "

11

JUMBLE®

Unscramble these four Jumbles, one letter to
each square, to form four ordinary words.

RODOB

NAFTI

LAYSIE

RELDEG

SHE'S A TEMPTINGLY
BEAUTIFUL WOMAN—
AND MIGHT DELIVER
A WARNING.

Now arrange the circled letters to form
the surprise answer, as suggested by the
above cartoon.

Print answer here

JUMBLE®

Unscramble these four Jumbles, one letter to each square, to form four ordinary words.

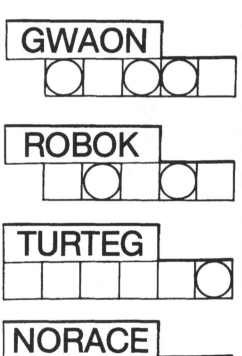

GWAON

ROBOK

TURTEG

NORACE

TO MAKE THIS, THE FARMER WORE A SHOE THAT WAS TOO TIGHT.

Now arrange the circled letters to form the surprise answer, as suggested by the above cartoon.

Print answer here HIS ⟨ ◯◯◯◯◯ ⟩ ⟨ ◯◯◯◯ ⟩

13

JUMBLE®

Unscramble these four Jumbles, one letter to
each square, to form four ordinary words.

UPPYP

LIFUD

REFIHE

SNORPE

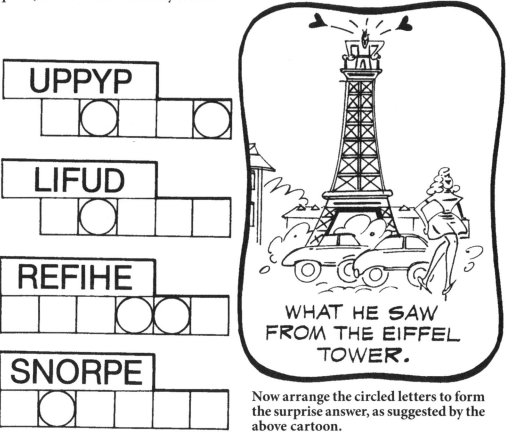

WHAT HE SAW
FROM THE EIFFEL
TOWER.

Now arrange the circled letters to form
the surprise answer, as suggested by the
above cartoon.

Print answer here AN " ⬡⬡⬡⬡⬡⬡ "

JUMBLE®

Unscramble these four Jumbles, one letter to
each square, to form four ordinary words.

ELVAT

TACHY

RAYSOV

CLISHE

WHAT THEY
CALLED THAT ACTOR
WHO ALWAYS PLAYED
THE VILLAIN.

Now arrange the circled letters to form
the surprise answer, as suggested by the
above cartoon.

Print
answer THE ⬡⬡⬡⬡⬡⬡ " ⬡⬡⬡⬡⬡⬡ "
here

JUMBLE®

Unscramble these four Jumbles, one letter to each square, to form four ordinary words.

CILRY

UNGTS

TANNIF

FIURAN

WHAT THE ORCHARD OWNER'S LIFE PROVED TO BE.

Now arrange the circled letters to form the surprise answer, as suggested by the above cartoon.

Print answer here VERY ◯◯◯◯◯◯◯◯

JUMBLE®

Unscramble these four Jumbles, one letter to
each square, to form four ordinary words.

NIRPT

KISLY

YALDDE

ORSOUP

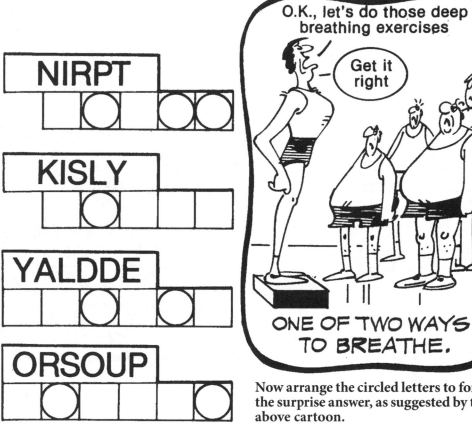

O.K., let's do those deep
breathing exercises

Get it
right

ONE OF TWO WAYS
TO BREATHE.

Now arrange the circled letters to form
the surprise answer, as suggested by the
above cartoon.

Print answer here

JUMBLE®

Unscramble these four Jumbles, one letter to each square, to form four ordinary words.

FUINY

RACZE

STEEWF

DORWAT

A-E-I-O-U

IT SEEMS RATHER FUNNY THAT ALL FIVE VOWELS APPEAR IN THIS WORD IN THEIR CORRECT ORDER.

Now arrange the circled letters to form the surprise answer, as suggested by the above cartoon.

Print answer here " ◯◯◯◯◯◯◯◯◯◯ "

JUMBLE®

Unscramble these four Jumbles, one letter to each square, to form four ordinary words.

OJYLL

FAHFC

CEEDDO

SPELTE

Ha ha—but they didn't get this ____

WHAT THE GUY WHO HID HIS WALLET IN THE FREEZER WAS LEFT WITH.

Now arrange the circled letters to form the surprise answer, as suggested by the above cartoon.

Print answer here ⬚⬚⬚⬚ ⬚⬚⬚⬚

JUMBLE®

Unscramble these four Jumbles, one letter to each square, to form four ordinary words.

LUSKK

GYLUL

BROJEB

GEAVAS

WHAT THOSE ANTS AT THE PICNIC DO.

Now arrange the circled letters to form the surprise answer, as suggested by the above cartoon.

Print answer here " ◯◯◯ " ◯◯

JUMBLE®

Unscramble these four Jumbles, one letter to each square, to form four ordinary words.

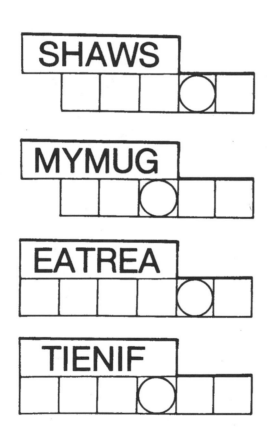

SHAWS

MYMUG

EATREA

TIENIF

Well, FINALLY we can predict sunshine

WHEN THE FOG CLEARS UP, IT WON'T BE THIS.

Now arrange the circled letters to form the surprise answer, as suggested by the above cartoon.

Print answer here "  "

JUMBLE®

Unscramble these four Jumbles, one letter to each square, to form four ordinary words.

LITTE

YASES

TENCED

ROMMIE

Very eligible — High class

WHAT A SUCCESSFUL BACHELOR DOES, WHICHEVER WAY YOU LOOK AT IT.

Now arrange the circled letters to form the surprise answer, as suggested by the above cartoon.

Print answer here " ◯◯◯◯◯◯ ◯◯◯◯◯◯◯ "

JUMBLE®

Unscramble these four Jumbles, one letter to each square, to form four ordinary words.

CEENI

RUTYL

VERGAN

DEGEWD

WHAT THE SWIMMING POOL CONTRACTOR DID WHEN BUSINESS FELL OFF.

Now arrange the circled letters to form the surprise answer, as suggested by the above cartoon.

Print answer here

JUMBLE®

Unscramble these four Jumbles, one letter to
each square, to form four ordinary words.

RYHUR

INVEG

DAJEGG

PACALA

AJAX
MILK
PRODUCTS
INC.

WHAT MANY EXPENSES
CONNECTED WITH THE
DAIRY BUSINESS
MIGHT BE.

Now arrange the circled letters to form
the surprise answer, as suggested by the
above cartoon.

Print answer here " ☐☐ ☐☐☐☐ "

JUMBLE®

Unscramble these four Jumbles, one letter to
each square, to form four ordinary words.

VACHO

SAUPE

TEMNEC

FLICEA

Let's do it again!

THEY ENJOYED THAT
VACATION IN THE SOUTH
PACIFIC SO MUCH THAT
THEY DECIDED TO GO
BACK FOR THIS.

Now arrange the circled letters to form
the surprise answer, as suggested by the
above cartoon.

Print answer here " ◯◯◯◯◯ "

JUMBLE®

Unscramble these four Jumbles, one letter to each square, to form four ordinary words.

VETEN

WAKOE

EISORE

SWEEFT

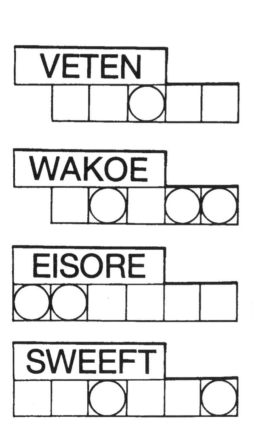

WHEN HE WENT ON THAT 14-DAY DIET, THIS WAS ALL HE LOST.

Now arrange the circled letters to form the surprise answer, as suggested by the above cartoon.

Print answer here

Lunar JUMBLE®

Daily Puzzles

JUMBLE®

Unscramble these four Jumbles, one letter to
each square, to form four ordinary words.

WEJEL

FEYHT

HIRTHE

IT'S GOOD MANNERS TO
TRY TO MAKE YOUR
GUESTS FEEL AT HOME,
ESPECIALLY WHEN
YOU WISH THIS.

ANTUSE

Now arrange the circled letters to form
the surprise answer, as suggested by the
above cartoon.

Print answer here

JUMBLE®

Unscramble these four Jumbles, one letter to
each square, to form four ordinary words.

FRUMO

NOIBS

CILIAT

WHARKE

HE FIDDLES WHILE
HIS LISTENERS
DO THIS.

Now arrange the circled letters to form
the surprise answer, as suggested by the
above cartoon.

Print answer here A

29

JUMBLE®

Unscramble these four Jumbles, one letter to
each square, to form four ordinary words.

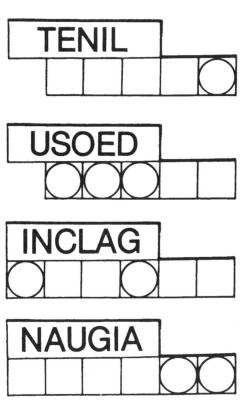

TENIL

USOED

INCLAG

NAUGIA

Look! A wonderful
job offer!

WHEN HIS SHIP
FINALLY CAME IN,
HE WAS TOO LAZY
TO DO THIS.

Now arrange the circled letters to form
the surprise answer, as suggested by the
above cartoon.

Print answer here

JUMBLE®

Unscramble these four Jumbles, one letter to
each square, to form four ordinary words.

REMIC

SELIA

ACCUST

TONKYT

Guess I'd better
bundle up

COULD IT BE A
RAINCOAT FOR WEAR
IN THE BIG TOWN?

Now arrange the circled letters to form
the surprise answer, as suggested by the
above cartoon.

Print
answer A ⃝⃝⃝⃝ ⃝⃝⃝⃝⃝⃝⃝
here

31

JUMBLE®

Unscramble these four Jumbles, one letter to
each square, to form four ordinary words.

ILEEX

SURVI

CLEMUS

CLAGEY

HOW FAR DOWN
WAS HER BATHING
SUIT CUT?

Now arrange the circled letters to form
the surprise answer, as suggested by the
above cartoon.

Print answer here   TO "◯◯◯" ◯◯◯◯◯◯

JUMBLE®

Unscramble these four Jumbles, one letter to
each square, to form four ordinary words.

CHEFT

RITTA

DEPENX

YURKET

WHAT HE AND
HIS GIRL WERE.

Now arrange the circled letters to form
the surprise answer, as suggested by the
above cartoon.

*Print answer
here*

JUMBLE®

Unscramble these four Jumbles, one letter to each square, to form four ordinary words.

PROOD

HIWEL

SLINUM

DRATOW

WHY THE BUSINESS TYCOON RUSHED OFF ON A MUCH NEEDED VACATION.

Now arrange the circled letters to form the surprise answer, as suggested by the above cartoon.

Print answer here TO ☐☐☐☐☐ ☐☐☐☐

JUMBLE®

Unscramble these four Jumbles, one letter to each square, to form four ordinary words.

GEFUD

EGUSS

WHARTT

GLOIBE

WHAT SOME WORK IN THE GARDEN CAN LEAVE ONE.

Now arrange the circled letters to form the surprise answer, as suggested by the above cartoon.

Print answer here "  "

35

JUMBLE®

Unscramble these four Jumbles, one letter to each square, to form four ordinary words.

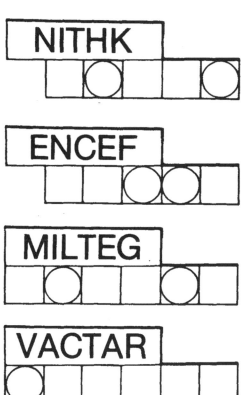

NITHK

ENCEF

MILTEG

VACTAR

SHOPPING CENTER
COST:
$48,000,000

REAL ESTATE

DON'T EXPECT SOME-ONE TO TALK TURKEY WHO'S THIS.

Now arrange the circled letters to form the surprise answer, as suggested by the above cartoon.

Print answer here

JUMBLE®

Unscramble these four Jumbles, one letter to
each square, to form four ordinary words.

CIEPE

YERAW

CHELEK

SATECK

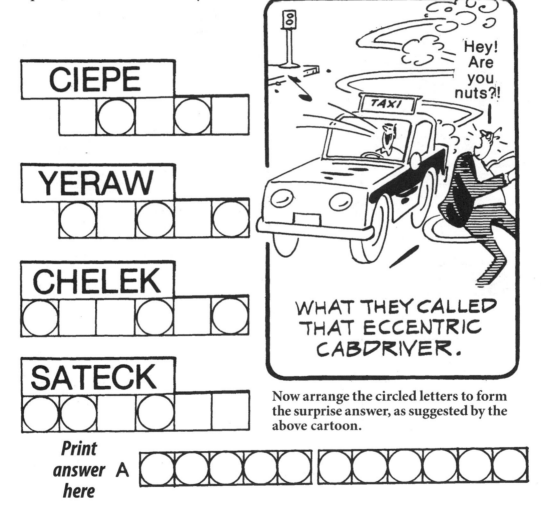

Hey!
Are
you
nuts?!

TAXI

WHAT THEY CALLED
THAT ECCENTRIC
CABDRIVER.

Now arrange the circled letters to form
the surprise answer, as suggested by the
above cartoon.

*Print
answer* A
here

JUMBLE®

Unscramble these four Jumbles, one letter to each square, to form four ordinary words.

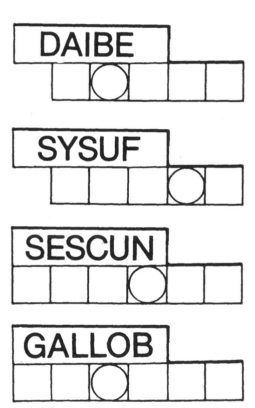

DAIBE

SYSUF

SESCUN

GALLOB

Here's the latest statement

You're not going to like it

PRESIDENT

WHAT THE BOSS WAS "BREAKING INTO."

Now arrange the circled letters to form the surprise answer, as suggested by the above cartoon.

Print answer here  " ◯◯◯◯ "

JUMBLE®

Unscramble these four Jumbles, one letter to
each square, to form four ordinary words.

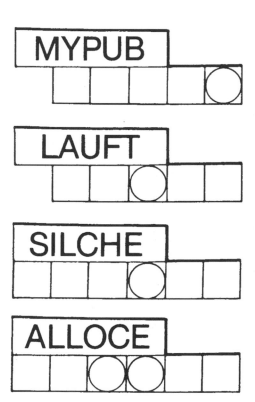

MYPUB

LAUFT

SILCHE

ALLOCE

HOW THE WAITRESS
ACTED WHEN SHE
SPILLED THE GRAVY.

Now arrange the circled letters to form
the surprise answer, as suggested by the
above cartoon.

Print answer here

39

JUMBLE®

Unscramble these four Jumbles, one letter to
each square, to form four ordinary words.

GLIVI

WYLEN

PANTIC

ABAANN

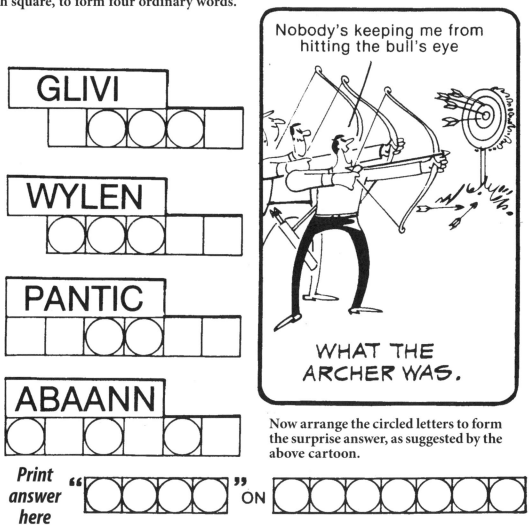

Nobody's keeping me from
hitting the bull's eye

WHAT THE
ARCHER WAS.

Now arrange the circled letters to form
the surprise answer, as suggested by the
above cartoon.

Print
answer
here

" ◯◯◯◯ " ON ◯◯◯◯◯◯◯◯◯

JUMBLE®

Unscramble these four Jumbles, one letter to
each square, to form four ordinary words.

HESOW

GAANP

URREBB

WOBETS

But I've looked everywhere

SUCH FRUIT IS
NOT CONSIDERED
MUCH GOOD WHEN
UNOBTAINABLE.

Now arrange the circled letters to form
the surprise answer, as suggested by the
above cartoon.

Print answer here

41

JUMBLE®

Unscramble these four Jumbles, one letter to
each square, to form four ordinary words.

YIFFT

TOBOY

MILDIP

REEBOF

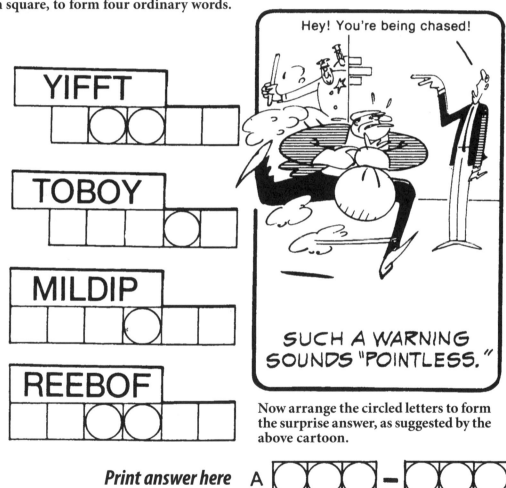

Hey! You're being chased!

SUCH A WARNING
SOUNDS "POINTLESS."

Now arrange the circled letters to form
the surprise answer, as suggested by the
above cartoon.

Print answer here A ◯◯◯ – ◯◯◯

JUMBLE®

Unscramble these four Jumbles, one letter to each square, to form four ordinary words.

SULPH

WYDON

CINDIT

SILFOS

Hey! Did I ever tell you about that night in Vegas?

COULD BE ALL THAT FIGHTER EVER LICKED.

Now arrange the circled letters to form the surprise answer, as suggested by the above cartoon.

Print answer here

JUMBLE®

Unscramble these four Jumbles, one letter to
each square, to form four ordinary words.

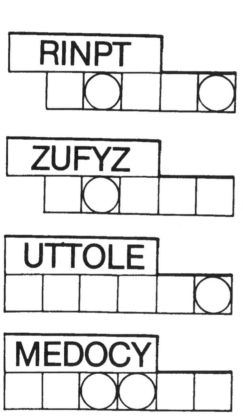

RINPT

ZUFYZ

UTTOLE

MEDOCY

COULD IT BE
A SOUND FROM
A DOG WITHOUT
A PEDIGREE?

Now arrange the circled letters to form
the surprise answer, as suggested by the
above cartoon.

Print answer here   A "⬡⬡⬡⬡ – ⬡⬡"

JUMBLE®

Unscramble these four Jumbles, one letter to
each square, to form four ordinary words.

YODIL

DIGUE

GLEMIN

TISSAD

WHAT THE ABSENT-
MINDED HEN DID.

Now arrange the circled letters to form
the surprise answer, as suggested by the
above cartoon.

**Print answer
here**

⬡⬡⬡⬡⬡⬡⬡ AN ⬡⬡⬡

JUMBLE®

Unscramble these four Jumbles, one letter to each square, to form four ordinary words.

ZIMEA

POAYS

SUNDOL

CUPSAM

MUSIC THAT MIGHT ACCOMPANY A TURKEY DINNER.

Now arrange the circled letters to form the surprise answer, as suggested by the above cartoon.

Print answer here A " ◯◯◯ " ◯◯◯◯◯◯◯◯

JUMBLE®

Unscramble these four Jumbles, one letter to
each square, to form four ordinary words.

CUROC

HIKKA

KORBEN

SOOPUR

HOW DOES THAT
FISHERMAN WHO
TENDS SHEEP ON
THE SIDE MAKE
A LIVING?

Now arrange the circled letters to form
the surprise answer, as suggested by the
above cartoon.

Print
answer BY ⬚⬚⬚⬚ OR BY ⬚⬚⬚⬚⬚⬚
here

JUMBLE®

Unscramble these four Jumbles, one letter to
each square, to form four ordinary words.

OPEEL

TOROB

SUSTLY

FUNCED

He just doesn't have
a green thumb

WHAT LIFE WAS
FOR THAT UNLUCKY
GARDENER.

Now arrange the circled letters to form
the surprise answer, as suggested by the
above cartoon.

**Print answer
here** NO

48

JUMBLE®

Unscramble these four Jumbles, one letter to each square, to form four ordinary words.

ALLIC

UPASE

STERJE

LYKING

HOW SHE FELT WHEN SHE ARRIVED HOME AFTER A SHOPPING BINGE.

Now arrange the circled letters to form the surprise answer, as suggested by the above cartoon.

Print answer here ⟨◯◯◯◯⟩ " ⟨◯◯◯◯◯◯⟩ "

JUMBLE®

Unscramble these four Jumbles, one letter to
each square, to form four ordinary words.

GROOF

OMPET

ATVARC

ENCHIL

You've had enough

BAR

WHAT KIND OF
PLANS WAS THE
ARCHITECT MAKING
FOR HIM?

Now arrange the circled letters to form
the surprise answer, as suggested by the
above cartoon.

Print answer here

JUMBLE®

Unscramble these four Jumbles, one letter to
each square, to form four ordinary words.

TANBO

DANGL

CONARY

VAHLED

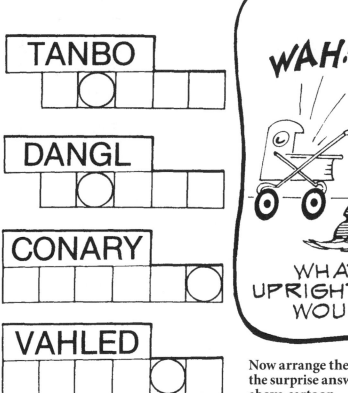

WAH!

WHAT NO
UPRIGHT PERSON
WOULD DO.

Now arrange the circled letters to form
the surprise answer, as suggested by the
above cartoon.

Print answer here

51

JUMBLE®

Unscramble these four Jumbles, one letter to each square, to form four ordinary words.

PORRI

VUEMA

GROFTE

TUCLED

Famous philosopher

WORDS YOU MIGHT GET FROM VOLTAIRE.

Now arrange the circled letters to form the surprise answer, as suggested by the above cartoon.

Print answer here " ☐ ☐☐☐☐ ☐☐☐ "

JUMBLE®

Unscramble these four Jumbles, one letter to each square, to form four ordinary words.

EUDES

SUGES

YAPNOC

DALLIP

Whew! That was close!

DID HANGMEN CARRY OUT SUCH SENTENCES?

Now arrange the circled letters to form the surprise answer, as suggested by the above cartoon.

Print answer here ⬡⬡⬡⬡⬡⬡⬡⬡⬡⬡ ONES

JUMBLE®

Unscramble these four Jumbles, one letter to
each square, to form four ordinary words.

TUDOO

OUSIP

NOOPUC

MUSSIE

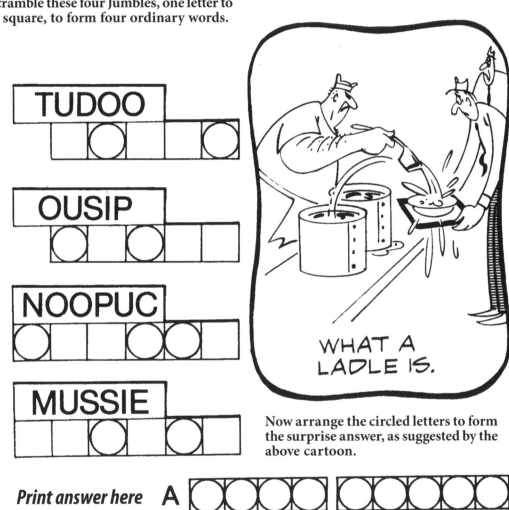

WHAT A
LADLE IS.

Now arrange the circled letters to form
the surprise answer, as suggested by the
above cartoon.

Print answer here A ⬜⬜⬜⬜⬜ ⬜⬜⬜⬜⬜⬜

JUMBLE®

Unscramble these four Jumbles, one letter to each square, to form four ordinary words.

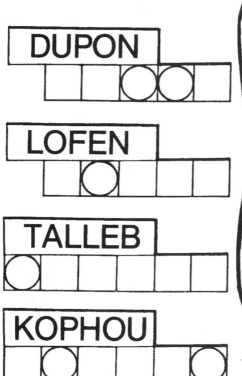

DUPON

LOFEN

TALLEB

KOPHOU

Got a stiff exam tomorrow

THE SKELETON WAS BURNING THE MID-NIGHT OIL BE-CAUSE HE WANTED TO DO THIS.

Now arrange the circled letters to form the surprise answer, as suggested by the above cartoon.

Print answer here

JUMBLE®

Unscramble these four Jumbles, one letter to each square, to form four ordinary words.

NILER

SUMIN

GARCHE

NAPMEN

METAL DEVICES THAT HELP KEEP LOCKS IN PLACE.

Now arrange the circled letters to form the surprise answer, as suggested by the above cartoon.

Print answer here

56

JUMBLE®

Unscramble these four Jumbles, one letter to
each square, to form four ordinary words.

SUMEA

ILETT

NILJEG

GAYMIB

WHAT A GIRL
SOMETIMES WEARS
AT THE BEACH.

Now arrange the circled letters to form
the surprise answer, as suggested by the
above cartoon.

*Print
answer
here* A

57

JUMBLE®

Unscramble these four Jumbles, one letter to
each square, to form four ordinary words.

TOUHY

FRUOM

SITMIF

CACTEN

Work when
you please

A JOB FOR
SOMEONE WHO'S
WELL-PADDED.

Now arrange the circled letters to form
the surprise answer, as suggested by the
above cartoon.

Print answer here " ⬭⬭⬭⬭⬭ "

58

JUMBLE®

Unscramble these four Jumbles, one letter to
each square, to form four ordinary words.

NERAV

VALIT

MEEGRE

SCIBEP

A FRUITFUL
SOURCE OF
INFORMATION.

Now arrange the circled letters to form
the surprise answer, as suggested by the
above cartoon.

Print answer here THE ☐☐☐☐☐☐☐☐☐☐☐☐

JUMBLE®

Unscramble these four Jumbles, one letter to
each square, to form four ordinary words.

NORPE

AVVLE

TRUFOH

SUCCAU

HOW THEY CLAPPED
THEIR HANDS WHEN
SHE SANG.

Now arrange the circled letters to form
the surprise answer, as suggested by the
above cartoon.

**Print answer
here** ◯◯◯◯ THEIR ◯◯◯◯

JUMBLE

Unscramble these four Jumbles, one letter to each square, to form four ordinary words.

ZIERP

CHALT

LETTOU

ABHORR

WHAT SHE HOPED
THE BACHELOR
WOULD DO ABOUT
HIS WAY OF LIFE.

Now arrange the circled letters to form the surprise answer, as suggested by the above cartoon.

Print answer here " ⬡⬡⬡⬡⬡ " ⬡⬡

61

JUMBLE®

Unscramble these four Jumbles, one letter to each square, to form four ordinary words.

BEREM

LIDAP

TEENAG

GLEANT

WHAT HE HAD TO DO EVERY TIME SHE HAD AN ACCIDENT IN THE KITCHEN.

Now arrange the circled letters to form the surprise answer, as suggested by the above cartoon.

Print answer here ☐☐☐☐ IT FOR ☐☐☐☐☐☐☐

JUMBLE®

Unscramble these four Jumbles, one letter to each square, to form four ordinary words.

LENEK
◯◯◯☐◯

GALUH
◯◯◯☐☐

BIMBIE
☐☐◯☐◯☐

KOJECY
☐☐◯☐◯☐

THEY CALLED HIM A COLORFUL FIGHTER BECAUSE HE WAS THIS MOST OF THE TIME.

Now arrange the circled letters to form the surprise answer, as suggested by the above cartoon.

Print answer here ◯◯◯◯◯ & ◯◯◯◯

JUMBLE®

Unscramble these four Jumbles, one letter to each square, to form four ordinary words.

CARTT

HOOPT

TYMINE

BRUBUS

WHAT A SOAP OPERA USUALLY IS.

Now arrange the circled letters to form the surprise answer, as suggested by the above cartoon.

Print answer here ☐☐☐☐ ON THE ☐☐☐

JUMBLE®

Unscramble these four Jumbles, one letter to each square, to form four ordinary words.

LYDIO

NEESU

WREABE

ICKEOO

WHAT THE PRETTY BLOND TEACHER WAS, AS DESCRIBED BY HER PUPILS.

Now arrange the circled letters to form the surprise answer, as suggested by the above cartoon.

Print answer here ⬡⬡⬡⬡ – ⬡⬡⬡⬡

JUMBLE®

Unscramble these four Jumbles, one letter to
each square, to form four ordinary words.

KARAP

FERIG

CENTEM

RYNTIG

WHAT'S THE BEST
AGE TO GET
HITCHED?

Now arrange the circled letters to form
the surprise answer, as suggested by the
above cartoon.

Print answer here " ◯◯◯◯◯ – ◯◯◯ "

JUMBLE®

Unscramble these four Jumbles, one letter to each square, to form four ordinary words.

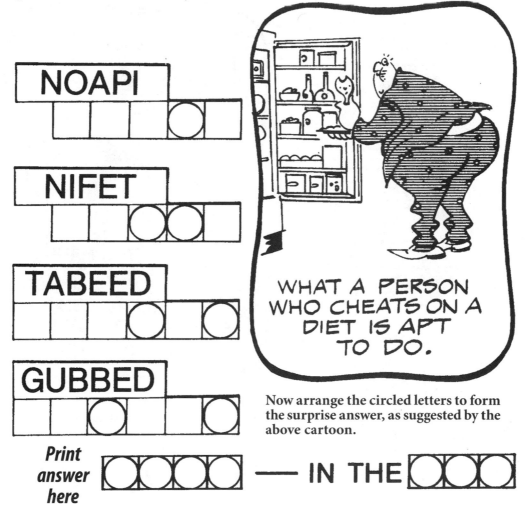

WHAT A PERSON WHO CHEATS ON A DIET IS APT TO DO.

NOAPI

NIFET

TABEED

GUBBED

Now arrange the circled letters to form the surprise answer, as suggested by the above cartoon.

Print answer here ◯◯◯◯ — IN THE ◯◯◯

67

JUMBLE

Unscramble these four Jumbles, one letter to each square, to form four ordinary words.

LANUN

MUJOB

PUNACK

TONPHY

Sure, I'll lend you the dough

WHAT AN HONEST ELEVATOR MAN PROBABLY IS.

Now arrange the circled letters to form the surprise answer, as suggested by the above cartoon.

Print answer here ◯◯ THE ◯◯ & ◯◯

JUMBLE®

Unscramble these four Jumbles, one letter to
each square, to form four ordinary words.

SBELS

DYRIT

GRIFIN

RODINO

TONITE
JONES VS. SMITH

IN THIS SITUATION,
YOU'LL BE VERY
CLOSE TO A
FIGHT.

Now arrange the circled letters to form
the surprise answer, as suggested by the
above cartoon.

Print answer here

JUMBLE®

Unscramble these four Jumbles, one letter to
each square, to form four ordinary words.

YACED
◻◻◯◻◻

SHOIT
◯◯◻◻◻

RAYATS
◻◯◻◻◯◻

BARKEY
◻◻◯◻◻◻

MIGHT BE
A CURRENT
SENSATION.

Now arrange the circled letters to form
the surprise answer, as suggested by the
above cartoon.

Print answer here ◻ ◯◯◯◯◯

JUMBLE®

Unscramble these four Jumbles, one letter to
each square, to form four ordinary words.

URPPE

LONBE

NASTEF

PHORTY

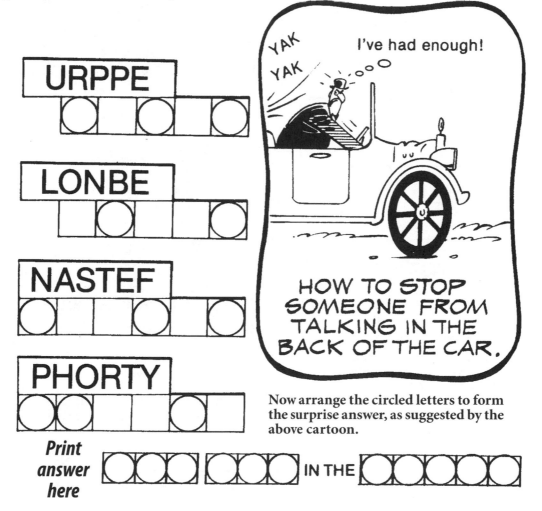

YAK
YAK

I've had enough!

HOW TO STOP
SOMEONE FROM
TALKING IN THE
BACK OF THE CAR.

Now arrange the circled letters to form
the surprise answer, as suggested by the
above cartoon.

Print
answer
here
⬡⬡⬡ ⬡⬡⬡ IN THE ⬡⬡⬡⬡⬡

JUMBLE®

Unscramble these four Jumbles, one letter to
each square, to form four ordinary words.

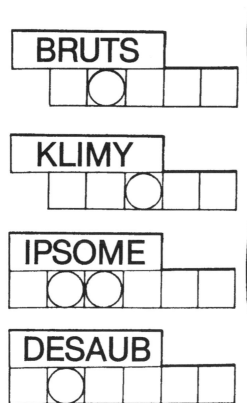

BRUTS

KLIMY

IPSOME

DESAUB

I always say honesty
is the best policy

YOU CAN PROVE
YOUR UPRIGHTNESS
BY TAKING
THIS LINE.

Now arrange the circled letters to form
the surprise answer, as suggested by the
above cartoon.

Print answer here ◯◯◯◯◯

JUMBLE®

Unscramble these four Jumbles, one letter to
each square, to form four ordinary words.

RAPEP

BLEAC

CINFAG

DALINS

IT'S NOT COMPLETELY
A "COLLAPSE"—
JUST THIS.

Now arrange the circled letters to form
the surprise answer, as suggested by the
above cartoon.

Print answer here ⬡ "⬡⬡⬡⬡⬡"

73

JUMBLE®

Unscramble these four Jumbles, one letter to each square, to form four ordinary words.

EAZUG

TAWLZ

BELMIN

GUSINE

I told you he'd call back if you just sat tight!

YOU NEED TO BIDE YOUR TIME TO PLAY THIS.

Now arrange the circled letters to form the surprise answer, as suggested by the above cartoon.

Print answer here   THE

JUMBLE®

Unscramble these four Jumbles, one letter to each square, to form four ordinary words.

POCHE

RAHME

STEACK

UMSOQE

MADE AN IMPRESSION ON THE BRIDLE PATH.

Now arrange the circled letters to form the surprise answer, as suggested by the above cartoon.

Print answer here A

JUMBLE®

Unscramble these four Jumbles, one letter to each square, to form four ordinary words.

DYNOW

YORRS

STELED

TRYSAP

SILENCE

Yak   Yak

WHAT A DICTIONARY NUT IS NEVER LIKELY TO BE.

Now arrange the circled letters to form the surprise answer, as suggested by the above cartoon.

Print answer here AT A ☐☐☐☐ FOR ☐☐☐☐☐☐

JUMBLE®

Unscramble these four Jumbles, one letter to
each square, to form four ordinary words.

UMPEL

BALFE

DOOHKE

TALCOE

COMES UNDER
PRESSURE WHEN
A DRIVER STEPS
ON IT.

Now arrange the circled letters to form
the surprise answer, as suggested by the
above cartoon.

Print answer here ◯◯◯ ◯◯◯◯◯◯.

JUMBLE®

Unscramble these four Jumbles, one letter to
each square, to form four ordinary words.

WECIT

CNOTH

DIRAHS

THOOSE

HOW FAR AWAY
DID DAVID STAND
FROM GOLIATH?

Now arrange the circled letters to form
the surprise answer, as suggested by the
above cartoon.

Print
answer A
here

JUMBLE®

Unscramble these four Jumbles, one letter to
each square, to form four ordinary words.

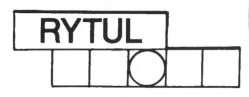

RYTUL

BYGAG

NAWSER

WETSOB

HOW THOSE
ARTILLERYMEN
WERE GOING.

Now arrange the circled letters to form
the surprise answer, as suggested by the
above cartoon.

Print answer here "◯◯◯◯◯ ◯◯◯◯"

JUMBLE®

Unscramble these four Jumbles, one letter to
each square, to form four ordinary words.

RAYRA

EPPIR

ENSCOD

HELSUB

WHAT SHE SAID
BAKING A GOOD
DESSERT WAS.

Now arrange the circled letters to form
the surprise answer, as suggested by the
above cartoon.

Print answer here

80

JUMBLE®

Unscramble these four Jumbles, one letter to
each square, to form four ordinary words.

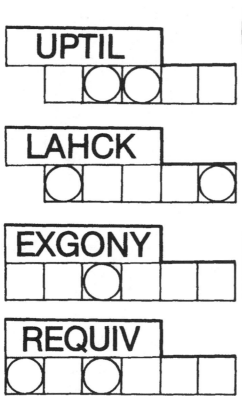

UPTIL

LAHCK

EXGONY

REQUIV

HOW TO DRESS
ON A VERY
COLD DAY.

Now arrange the circled letters to form
the surprise answer, as suggested by the
above cartoon.

Print answer here

JUMBLE®

Unscramble these four Jumbles, one letter to
each square, to form four ordinary words.

SETAC

ENMOY

WHYNOA

DILBOE

WHY THE COPS
COULDN'T CATCH
UP WITH THE
PICKPOCKET.

Now arrange the circled letters to form
the surprise answer, as suggested by the
above cartoon.

Print answer here HE ⃝⃝⃝⃝⃝⃝ ⃝⃝⃝⃝

JUMBLE®

Unscramble these four Jumbles, one letter to
each square, to form four ordinary words.

LEBER

VELGA

SOUTID

BRATIB

WHAT THEY SAID
THE DYNAMITERS'
ANNUAL SHINDIG
WAS.

Now arrange the circled letters to form
the surprise answer, as suggested by the
above cartoon.

Print answer here A

JUMBLE

Unscramble these four Jumbles, one letter to each square, to form four ordinary words.

GEGAU

CYKAT

QUORIL

VERABE

NO, HE WAS NOT AFTER THE FAMILY PET.

Now arrange the circled letters to form the surprise answer, as suggested by the above cartoon.

Print answer here THE 〇〇〇〇 〇〇〇〇〇〇〇〇〇

JUMBLE®

Unscramble these four Jumbles, one letter to each square, to form four ordinary words.

LEERD

BLAWR

MURQUO

AURBUE

i'm getting hungry

COULD MAKE ONE THINK OF FOOD— A LINE OF MEN WAITING FOR HAIRCUTS.

Now arrange the circled letters to form the surprise answer, as suggested by the above cartoon.

Print answer here

" ⬡⬡⬡⬡⬡⬡ ⬡⬡⬡⬡⬡ "

JUMBLE®

Unscramble these four Jumbles, one letter to each square, to form four ordinary words.

LIBOR

HEWEL

CORNEE

MOTELE

WHAT THAT NEWCOMER MADE.

Now arrange the circled letters to form the surprise answer, as suggested by the above cartoon.

Print answer here " ⬡⬡⬡ ⬡⬡⬡⬡⬡ "

JUMBLE®

Unscramble these four Jumbles, one letter to
each square, to form four ordinary words.

CHUGO

ATING

LANNID

GLEIMN

THIS IS THE KEY
TO ALL GOOD
DRIVING.

Now arrange the circled letters to form
the surprise answer, as suggested by the
above cartoon.

Print answer here

JUMBLE®

Unscramble these four Jumbles, one letter to
each square, to form four ordinary words.

DARAW

COUNE

GROHPE

NORBIN

MIGHT PROVIDE
SOME REST FOR
A TIRED FISH.

Now arrange the circled letters to form
the surprise answer, as suggested by the
above cartoon.

Print answer here THE ◯◯◯◯◯◯ ◯◯◯

JUMBLE®

Unscramble these four Jumbles, one letter to
each square, to form four ordinary words.

NOMEW

CUJIE

SWAALY

BRICKE

Ugh!

WHAT THOSE
HOBOES WERE
TELLING.

Now arrange the circled letters to form
the surprise answer, as suggested by the
above cartoon.

Print answer here " ⬡⬡⬡ " ⬡⬡⬡⬡⬡

JUMBLE®

Unscramble these four Jumbles, one letter to
each square, to form four ordinary words.

NOJAB

CLECY

HARSHT

CEEDIT

WHAT THE MAN WHO
INVENTED THE SLIDE
FASTENER HOPED
IT WOULD DO.

Now arrange the circled letters to form
the surprise answer, as suggested by the
above cartoon.

Print answer here "◯◯◯◯◯ ◯◯"

90

JUMBLE®

Unscramble these four Jumbles, one letter to each square, to form four ordinary words.

INEEC

BIELL

GORUBE

HERTAH

NOT THE WHOLE STORY OF LADY GODIVA — JUST THIS.

Now arrange the circled letters to form the surprise answer, as suggested by the above cartoon.

Print answer here

A " ⬡⬡⬡⬡ " ⬡⬡⬡⬡⬡⬡⬡⬡

JUMBLE®

Unscramble these four Jumbles, one letter to
each square, to form four ordinary words.

WORNC

SQUET

DRAFTI

FRYLUR

It'll sell a
million records

WHAT TUNE MAKES
A PERFORMER
HAPPY?

Now arrange the circled letters to form
the surprise answer, as suggested by the
above cartoon.

Print answer here A " ☐☐☐ - ☐☐☐☐ "

JUMBLE®

Unscramble these four Jumbles, one letter to
each square, to form four ordinary words.

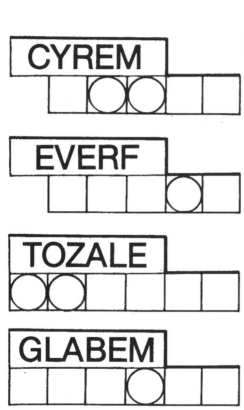

CYREM

EVERF

TOZALE

GLABEM

It's easy

WHAT SAILING A
BOAT MIGHT BE FOR
AN EXPERIENCED
SAILOR.

Now arrange the circled letters to form
the surprise answer, as suggested by the
above cartoon.

Print answer here A " ⬡⬡⬡⬡⬡⬡ "

JUMBLE®

Unscramble these four Jumbles, one letter to each square, to form four ordinary words.

HOPNY

YURMM

UNMAUT

NAFELL

WIN   PLACE

ON WHICH HE PLACED MONEY OF A CERTAIN AMOUNT.

Now arrange the circled letters to form the surprise answer, as suggested by the above cartoon.

Print answer here

JUMBLE®

Unscramble these four Jumbles, one letter to
each square, to form four ordinary words.

MILOB

DAAMM

BUHSIL

PIMAGE

WHERE IT COULD
BE SAID AT A
BANQUET.

Now arrange the circled letters to form
the surprise answer, as suggested by the
above cartoon.

Print answer here THE "⃝⃝⃝⃝"

JUMBLE®

Unscramble these four Jumbles, one letter to each square, to form four ordinary words.

REQUE

GRABE

JURNIY

DORCEF

WHAT THE HEAVY
SMOKER WAS
ADVISED TO DO.

Now arrange the circled letters to form the surprise answer, as suggested by the above cartoon.

Print answer here

JUMBLE®

Unscramble these four Jumbles, one letter to
each square, to form four ordinary words.

WARFE

YAIRN

DURSTY

THORCC

DUE FOR A
"ROASTING" FROM
THE SERGEANT.

Now arrange the circled letters to form
the surprise answer, as suggested by the
above cartoon.

Print
answer
here

A "⬡⬡⬡" ⬡⬡⬡⬡⬡⬡⬡

JUMBLE®

Unscramble these four Jumbles, one letter to
each square, to form four ordinary words.

FLAIN

KOWEA

PLOATS

LARREB

Don't believe
a word of it

COULD BE THE
RESULT OF
SPINNING A LOT
OF TALES.

Now arrange the circled letters to form
the surprise answer, as suggested by the
above cartoon.

Print answer here A

JUMBLE®

Unscramble these four Jumbles, one letter to each square, to form four ordinary words.

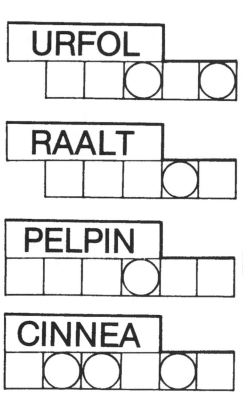

URFOL

RAALT

PELPIN

CINNEA

You're all in for a big surprise!

FOR SOMEONE WHO PLANS TO MAKE A SPLASH IN THE KITCHEN.

Now arrange the circled letters to form the surprise answer, as suggested by the above cartoon.

Print answer here

JUMBLE®

Unscramble these four Jumbles, one letter to each square, to form four ordinary words.

ROWBE

KNALF

RATHEG

DIFLED

Someday he'll own the paper

STILL A STUDENT—BUT HE HAS WITHIN HIM THE ABILITY TO MAKE MONEY.

Now arrange the circled letters to form the surprise answer, as suggested by the above cartoon.

Print answer here A " ☐ – ☐☐☐☐☐☐ "

100

JUMBLE

Unscramble these four Jumbles, one letter to
each square, to form four ordinary words.

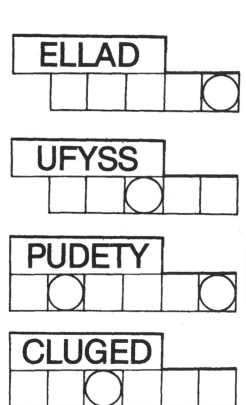

ELLAD

UFYSS

PUDETY

CLUGED

Get cleaned up—
we're expecting
company

HOW HE LOOKED
AFTER SPENDING
THE WHOLE DAY
PLANTING THE
GARDEN.

Now arrange the circled letters to form
the surprise answer, as suggested by the
above cartoon.

Print answer here " ⬡⬡⬡⬡⬡ "

101

JUMBLE®

Unscramble these four Jumbles, one letter to each square, to form four ordinary words.

TIPEY

HOTUM

WEENST

GRONTS

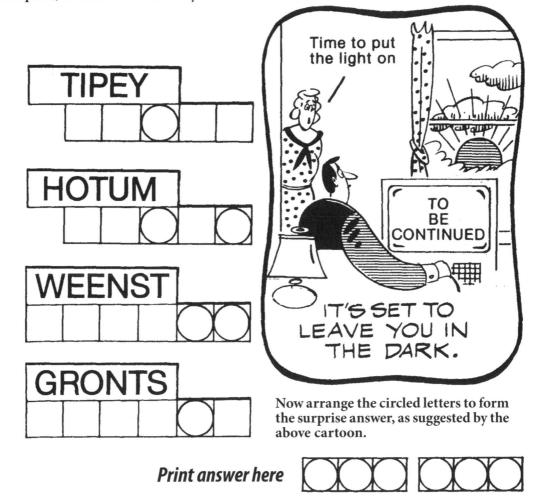

Time to put the light on

TO BE CONTINUED

IT'S SET TO LEAVE YOU IN THE DARK.

Now arrange the circled letters to form the surprise answer, as suggested by the above cartoon.

Print answer here

JUMBLE®

Unscramble these four Jumbles, one letter to each square, to form four ordinary words.

NIGLY

SEERA

DELIRB

DULCED

OBVIOUSLY NOT A
FLY-BY-NIGHT.

Now arrange the circled letters to form the surprise answer, as suggested by the above cartoon.

Print answer here THE ⬡⬡⬡⬡⬡ ⬡⬡⬡⬡

JUMBLE®

Unscramble these four Jumbles, one letter to each square, to form four ordinary words.

POATI

DESET

CUSSEN

ZERBAL

SUGGESTED THAT HE WAS PROUD OF THE FACT THAT HE WORKED LESS THAN ANYONE ELSE.

Now arrange the circled letters to form the surprise answer, as suggested by the above cartoon.

Print answer here AN ⬡⬡⬡⬡⬡ ⬡⬡⬡⬡⬡⬡

JUMBLE®

Unscramble these four Jumbles, one letter to
each square, to form four ordinary words.

SOUHE

ENATE

SHRAIG

GINCHA

WHAT ONE MOUSE
SAID TO THE OTHER
AS HE SAW THE TRAP
BEING BAITED.

Now arrange the circled letters to form
the surprise answer, as suggested by the
above cartoon.

Print answer here " ☐☐☐☐☐☐ ☐☐ "

JUMBLE®

Unscramble these four Jumbles, one letter to each square, to form four ordinary words.

DRY
CLEANER

AN ARTICLE OF
CLOTHING A GENTLE-
MAN MIGHT HAVE
AROUND THE ARM.

VINEA

MAROA

RAPTYN

CRALIG

Now arrange the circled letters to form the surprise answer, as suggested by the above cartoon.

Print answer here " ◯ – ◯◯◯ – ◯◯◯ "

JUMBLE®

Unscramble these four Jumbles, one letter to
each square, to form four ordinary words.

FRATE

EKRIP

JYLFOU

LAMTEL

WHAT THE GAMBLER
NAMED HIS
DAUGHTER.

Now arrange the circled letters to form
the surprise answer, as suggested by the
above cartoon.

Print answer here

JUMBLE®

Unscramble these four Jumbles, one letter to
each square, to form four ordinary words.

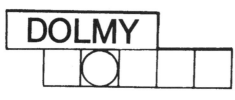

DOLMY

TORIB

YAHRLD

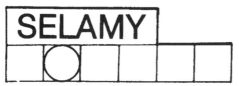

SELAMY

RAN OFF WITH
A ROLL OF
CLOTH.

Now arrange the circled letters to form
the surprise answer, as suggested by the
above cartoon.

Print answer here "◯◯◯◯◯ – ◯◯"

108

JUMBLE®

Unscramble these four Jumbles, one letter to
each square, to form four ordinary words.

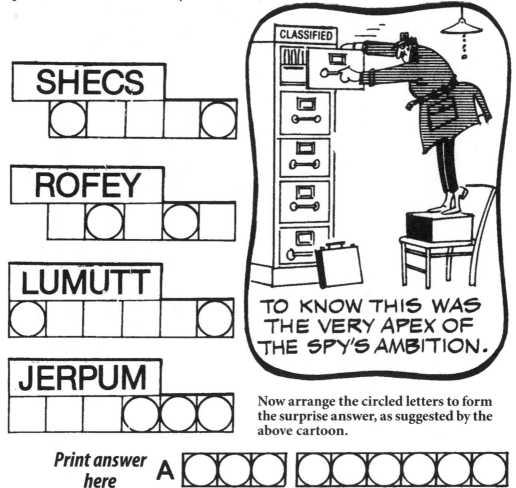

SHECS

ROFEY

LUMUTT

JERPUM

CLASSIFIED

TO KNOW THIS WAS
THE VERY APEX OF
THE SPY'S AMBITION.

Now arrange the circled letters to form
the surprise answer, as suggested by the
above cartoon.

**Print answer
here** A ☐☐☐ ☐☐☐☐☐☐

JUMBLE®

Unscramble these four Jumbles, one letter to
each square, to form four ordinary words.

LUBLY

WOLLY

FARIDA

VELENE

THE SORT OF LIFE
YOU MIGHT EXPECT A
GLUTTON TO LEAD.

Now arrange the circled letters to form
the surprise answer, as suggested by the
above cartoon.

Print answer here A ⃝⃝⃝⃝ ⃝⃝⃝

JUMBLE®

Unscramble these four Jumbles, one letter to
each square, to form four ordinary words.

THACC

LIDAY

TURBAP

DEEMLY

WHERE'S THE MOST
DIFFICULT LOCK
TO PICK?

Now arrange the circled letters to form
the surprise answer, as suggested by the
above cartoon.

Print answer here ON A ☐☐☐☐ ☐☐☐☐

JUMBLE®

Unscramble these four Jumbles, one letter to
each square, to form four ordinary words.

I hear he's a member
of the nobility

A TITLE THE
BOXER DIDN'T
AIM TO BE
OUT FOR.

TYMUS

NOPEY

GINENE

RYBBAC

Now arrange the circled letters to form
the surprise answer, as suggested by the
above cartoon.

Print answer here " ◯◯◯◯◯ "

JUMBLE®

Unscramble these four Jumbles, one letter to each square, to form four ordinary words.

SIPOE

DUNTE

CHOSOL

KRILLE

Oh, NOW I get it!

WHEN IS A JOKE MOST EFFECTIVE?

Now arrange the circled letters to form the surprise answer, as suggested by the above cartoon.

Print answer here   WHEN IT

JUMBLE®

Unscramble these four Jumbles, one letter to
each square, to form four ordinary words.

NARCK
[ ][ ](○)(○)[ ]

PHULS
[ ][ ][ ](○)(○)

TIXECE
[ ][ ][ ][ ](○)[ ]

UNCOBE
[ ](○)[ ](○)[ ](○)(○)

THE "DISINTE-
GRATION" OF ONE
STAR MAY THREATEN
THE WHOLE NATION.

Now arrange the circled letters to form
the surprise answer, as suggested by the
above cartoon.

Print answer here " (○)(○)(○)(○)(○)(○)(○) "

JUMBLE®

Unscramble these four Jumbles, one letter to each square, to form four ordinary words.

SNALT

OOCCA

SWEDIT

THIMER

MOST DUELS ARE RATHER SHORT AFFAIRS BECAUSE THEY ONLY REQUIRE THIS.

Now arrange the circled letters to form the surprise answer, as suggested by the above cartoon.

Print answer here

JUMBLE®

Unscramble these four Jumbles, one letter to
each square, to form four ordinary words.

VCFAR

NUF.QE

LAIWHE

RETAIS

NOT A BAD THING TO DO WHEN IN COURT.

Now arrange the circled letters to form
the surprise answer, as suggested by the
above cartoon.

Print answer here

JUMBLE®

Unscramble these four Jumbles, one letter to
each square, to form four ordinary words.

GIREM

VANEH

TUFLAR

HUGNOE

WHAT WAS THE
NEW BRIDE'S
FAVORITE FISH?

Now arrange the circled letters to form
the surprise answer, as suggested by the
above cartoon.

Print answer here " ⬡⬡⬡ – ⬡⬡⬡⬡ "

JUMBLE®

Unscramble these four Jumbles, one letter to each square, to form four ordinary words.

URIOC

ZEFOR

DRAACE

NOLEST

Aha!

WHAT HE HAD ON AS A RESULT OF GETTING INTO A PICKLE.

Now arrange the circled letters to form the surprise answer, as suggested by the above cartoon.

Print answer here A ⬡⬡⬡⬡ ⬡⬡⬡⬡

JUMBLE®

Unscramble these four Jumbles, one letter to each square, to form four ordinary words.

PRUSN

HOPUC

ROTRAM

HISVAL

COULD THEY BE CHISELERS EMPLOYED ON "RELIEF" PROJECTS?

Now arrange the circled letters to form the surprise answer, as suggested by the above cartoon.

Print answer here

119

JUMBLE®

Unscramble these four Jumbles, one letter to
each square, to form four ordinary words.

TADAP

LEWJE

TRAULB

NACAMI

THERE MAY BE A
FORTUNE TO BE
FOUND AT THE BOTTOM
OF THIS VESSEL.

Now arrange the circled letters to form
the surprise answer, as suggested by the
above cartoon.

Print answer here A ⬡⬡⬡⬡⬡⬡⬡

120

JUMBLE®

Unscramble these four Jumbles, one letter to each square, to form four ordinary words.

LOBOD

TAGOL

VIPSEL

HOIDAR

THE WORLD'S BIGGEST HOLD-UP MAN.

Now arrange the circled letters to form the surprise answer, as suggested by the above cartoon.

Print answer here

JUMBLE®

Unscramble these four Jumbles, one letter to each square, to form four ordinary words.

SIGEE

RUSIV

POTTIE

REDOBT

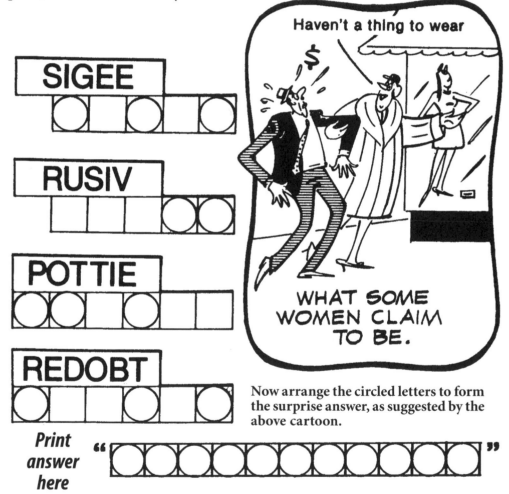

Haven't a thing to wear

WHAT SOME
WOMEN CLAIM
TO BE.

Now arrange the circled letters to form the surprise answer, as suggested by the above cartoon.

Print answer here " "

JUMBLE®

Unscramble these four Jumbles, one letter to each square, to form four ordinary words.

RYPEK

SINBO

YAUNES

KALTEC

LOOKS AT THEM
COMING AND GOING—
IN BOTH
DIRECTIONS.

Now arrange the circled letters to form the surprise answer, as suggested by the above cartoon.

Print answer here

JUMBLE®

Unscramble these four Jumbles, one letter to each square, to form four ordinary words.

TARFD

CAMPH

SPICHY

TENCIE

You're wonderful!

Yes, I know

WHAT THAT "SWELL" GUY HAD.

Now arrange the circled letters to form the surprise answer, as suggested by the above cartoon.

Print answer here   A ⃝⃝⃝⃝ TO ⃝⃝⃝⃝⃝

JUMBLE®

Unscramble these four Jumbles, one letter to each square, to form four ordinary words.

REEMY

DRIPA

SLOIPH

CLEMPO

HOW DO YOU ARRIVE AT THE TOP OF A CHURCH STEEPLE ON A HOT DAY?

Now arrange the circled letters to form the surprise answer, as suggested by the above cartoon.

Print answer here "☐◯◯◯☐ - ☐◯◯◯◯◯☐"

125

JUMBLE®

Unscramble these four Jumbles, one letter to
each square, to form four ordinary words.

AXORB

KEDAC

DUBACT

KUBECT

I told you so

WHAT GARDENING
THAT BEGINS AT
DAYBREAK OFTEN
ENDS UP WITH.

Now arrange the circled letters to form
the surprise answer, as suggested by the
above cartoon.

Print answer here " "

JUMBLE®

Unscramble these four Jumbles, one letter to
each square, to form four ordinary words.

STRUY

COPAH

AJURAG

DUCINE

Must
be nuts!

CLICK!

WHAT PEOPLE
WHO CUT YOU SHORT
ON THE PHONE
EVIDENTLY HAVE.

Now arrange the circled letters to form
the surprise answer, as suggested by the
above cartoon.

Print answer here ◯◯◯◯ – ◯◯◯

JUMBLE®

Unscramble these four Jumbles, one letter to
each square, to form four ordinary words.

DALGE

ATTIR

GORUME

CANVAT

A **GREAT OVEN** MIGHT PRODUCE MOST OF THIS.

Now arrange the circled letters to form
the surprise answer, as suggested by the
above cartoon.

Print answer " "
here

JUMBLE®

Unscramble these four Jumbles, one letter to
each square, to form four ordinary words.

OVEEK

SHUBY

CEADED

KILLEY

VEGETABLES THAT
SOUND AS THOUGH
THEY SHOULD
NEVER BE SERVED
ABOARD SHIP.

Now arrange the circled letters to form
the surprise answer, as suggested by the
above cartoon.

Print answer here

129

JUMBLE®

Unscramble these four Jumbles, one letter to
each square, to form four ordinary words.

UNDAT

ORNOC

FINTEC

TULFAY

HUFF   PUFF   PUFF

WHAT SOME
JOGGERS
TEND TO DO.

Now arrange the circled letters to form
the surprise answer, as suggested by the
above cartoon.

Print answer here

JUMBLE®

Unscramble these four Jumbles, one letter to each square, to form four ordinary words.

LAIGY

YIHFS

KLEETT

MIRAPI

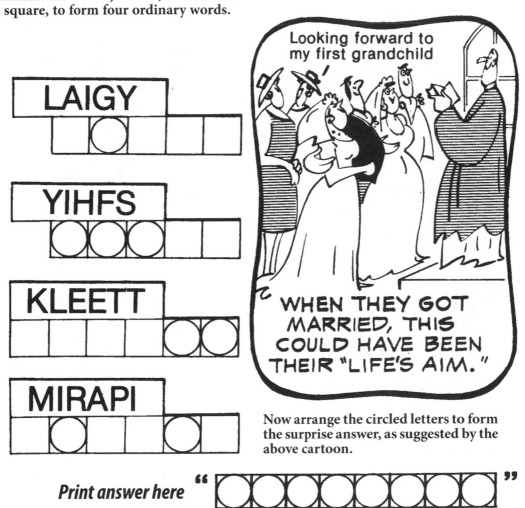

Looking forward to my first grandchild

WHEN THEY GOT MARRIED, THIS COULD HAVE BEEN THEIR "LIFE'S AIM."

Now arrange the circled letters to form the surprise answer, as suggested by the above cartoon.

Print answer here "◯◯◯◯◯◯◯◯◯"

131

JUMBLE®

Unscramble these four Jumbles, one letter to each square, to form four ordinary words.

VOABE

KNACS

ENMURB

FUNIES

Now arrange the circled letters to form the surprise answer, as suggested by the above cartoon.

Print answer here A ⬡⬡⬡⬡ ⬡⬡⬡⬡⬡⬡

JUMBLE®

Unscramble these four Jumbles, one letter to each square, to form four ordinary words.

ZYZID

RIQUE

RETAIW

UNRICH

A snap

WHAT A BRIGHT STUDENT IS EXPECTED TO DO WHEN THERE'S AN EXAM.

Now arrange the circled letters to form the surprise answer, as suggested by the above cartoon.

Print answer here

◯◯◯◯ THROUGH THE ◯◯◯◯

JUMBLE®

Unscramble these four Jumbles, one letter to
each square, to form four ordinary words.

GULIE

NOANY

DIBORM

OOLANG

THIS MATERIAL
NEVER GETS
WORN OUT.

Now arrange the circled letters to form
the surprise answer, as suggested by the
above cartoon.

Print answer here

JUMBLE.

Unscramble these four Jumbles, one letter to
each square, to form four ordinary words.

IBARR

SOGEO

FARFAY

GEDDUR

A BIG WHEEL IN
THE AMUSEMENT
BUSINESS.

Now arrange the circled letters to form
the surprise answer, as suggested by the
above cartoon.

Print answer here

JUMBLE®

Unscramble these four Jumbles, one letter to
each square, to form four ordinary words.

WONIG

HILEW

RALOPP

LESCUM

For the
old man

Shhh

THE GENERAL'S
FAVORITE
HEADQUARTERS.

Now arrange the circled letters to form
the surprise answer, as suggested by the
above cartoon.

Print answer here ⬡⬡⬡ ⬡⬡⬡⬡⬡⬡

136

JUMBLE®

Unscramble these four Jumbles, one letter to
each square, to form four ordinary words.

INGGO

KLUFE

FLABEL

CLARRO

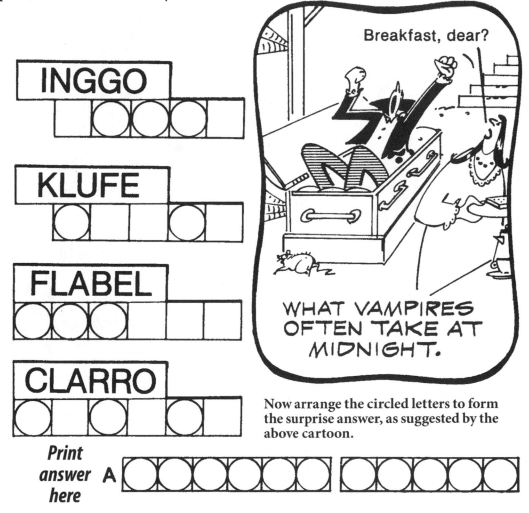

Breakfast, dear?

WHAT VAMPIRES
OFTEN TAKE AT
MIDNIGHT.

Now arrange the circled letters to form
the surprise answer, as suggested by the
above cartoon.

Print
answer
here

A

JUMBLE®

Unscramble these four Jumbles, one letter to
each square, to form four ordinary words.

NOVEM
◯ □ □ □ ◯

YURRC
□ □ ◯ □ □

PRAUPE
□ □ □ □ ◯ ◯

ENFLOY
□ ◯ □ ◯ □ □

HOW TO MAKE
VARNISH DISAPPEAR.

Now arrange the circled letters to form
the surprise answer, as suggested by the
above cartoon.

Print answer here ◯◯◯◯◯◯ THE ◯

JUMBLE®

Unscramble these four Jumbles, one letter to each square, to form four ordinary words.

TOIDI

DEWEG

RORTER

COLUSH

WHAT THAT FAMOUS AUTHOR BECAME AFTER HE PASSED AWAY.

Now arrange the circled letters to form the surprise answer, as suggested by the above cartoon.

Print answer here A " ⬡⬡⬡⬡⬡ " ⬡⬡⬡⬡⬡⬡

JUMBLE®

Unscramble these four Jumbles, one letter to each square, to form four ordinary words.

CHEEN
◯◯◯◯◯

SMIPK
◯◯◯◯◯

MEEDAF
◯◯◯◯◯◯

HEETES
◯◯◯◯◯◯

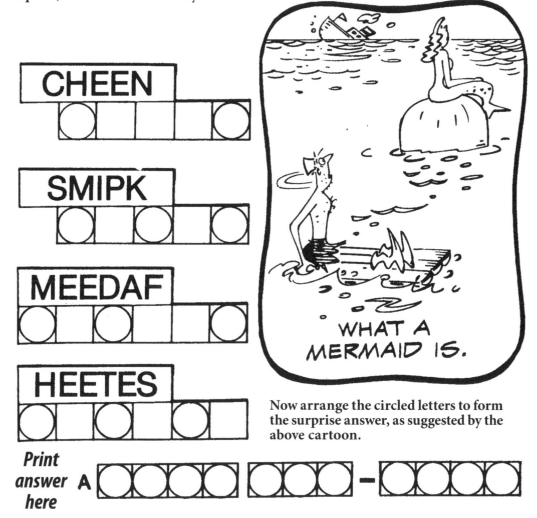

WHAT A MERMAID IS.

Now arrange the circled letters to form the surprise answer, as suggested by the above cartoon.

Print answer here A ◯◯◯◯◯ ◯◯◯ – ◯◯◯◯◯

JUMBLE

Unscramble these four Jumbles, one letter to
each square, to form four ordinary words.

NYWEL

GLARN

MILTEY

BUSTIM

Nothing for me

YOU MIGHT SERVE
IT TO OTHERS, BUT
YOU WOULDN'T WANT TO
EAT IT YOURSELF.

Now arrange the circled letters to form
the surprise answer, as suggested by the
above cartoon.

Print answer
here

A ⬜⬜⬜⬜⬜⬜⬜ ⬜⬜⬜⬜

JUMBLE®

Unscramble these four Jumbles, one letter to
each square, to form four ordinary words.

VELOR

DIOTT

SEVURS

HARMIO

HONK
HONK
HONK
SPUTTER

WHAT A SOUPED-UP
CAR THAT BROKE
DOWN WAS.

Now arrange the circled letters to form
the surprise answer, as suggested by the
above cartoon.

Print answer here   A " ⃝⃝⃝⃝⃝ " ⃝⃝⃝

JUMBLE®

Unscramble these four Jumbles, one letter to
each square, to form four ordinary words.

IRROG

GUBOH

KEENAW

DYLOOB

SILENCE

WHY THE BOOKWORM
VISITED THE
LIBRARY.

Now arrange the circled letters to form
the surprise answer, as suggested by the
above cartoon.

Print
answer TO "⎕⎕⎕⎕⎕⎕⎕" A ⎕⎕⎕⎕
here

143

JUMBLE®

Unscramble these four Jumbles, one letter to
each square, to form four ordinary words.

TCHEF

LATAN

NICCIP

DUNTIC

WHERE YOU'RE APT
TO FIND THE
MOST FISH.

Now arrange the circled letters to form
the surprise answer, as suggested by the
above cartoon.

Print answer here BETWEEN ⬭⬭⬭⬭⬭ & ⬭⬭⬭⬭⬭

JUMBLE®

Unscramble these four Jumbles, one letter to
each square, to form four ordinary words.

INORM

ETTEW

GITSAM

STUCCA

QXXX-TV
W CASTING FOR
NEW SERIES

My uncle's
the producer

AN EASY WAY TO
GET ON TV.

Now arrange the circled letters to form
the surprise answer, as suggested by the
above cartoon.

Print answer here ◯◯◯ ◯◯ YOUR ◯◯◯

145

JUMBLE®

Unscramble these four Jumbles, one letter to
each square, to form four ordinary words.

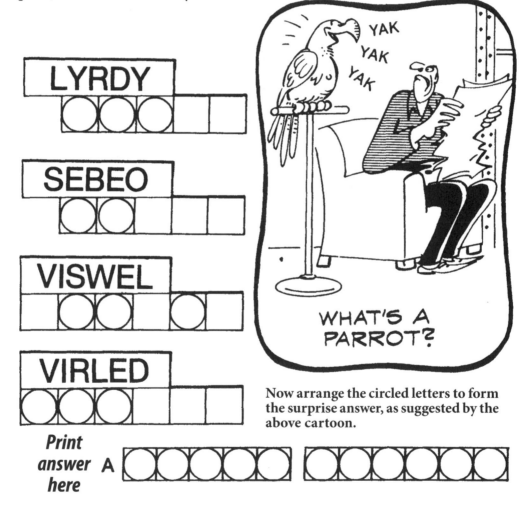

LYRDY

SEBEO

VISWEL

VIRLED

YAK
YAK
YAK

WHAT'S A
PARROT?

Now arrange the circled letters to form
the surprise answer, as suggested by the
above cartoon.

Print
answer A
here

JUMBLE®

Unscramble these four Jumbles, one letter to
each square, to form four ordinary words.

PETIR

HORAC

BIRDHY

ROTTET

Can't it be turned off?

WHAT **THE RADIATOR** PRODUCED.

Now arrange the circled letters to form
the surprise answer, as suggested by the
above cartoon.

Print
answer
here

"A ⬡⬡⬡⬡⬡⬡⬡ ⬡⬡⬡⬡"

JUMBLE®

Unscramble these four Jumbles, one letter to
each square, to form four ordinary words.

LOCCI

OSKET

GUBLIN

NORIPS

WHAT THE
REFRIGERATOR DID
DURING THE POWER
FAILURE.

Now arrange the circled letters to form
the surprise answer, as suggested by the
above cartoon.

Print answer here ⬡⬡⬡⬡⬡ ITS ⬡⬡⬡⬡⬡

JUMBLE®

Unscramble these four Jumbles, one letter to
each square, to form four ordinary words.

RUSUY

YOULS

NOMOAR

UPGLEN

WON FIRST PRIZE
AT THE CAT SHOW.

Now arrange the circled letters to form
the surprise answer, as suggested by the
above cartoon.

*Print
answer A
here*

149

JUMBLE®

Unscramble these four Jumbles, one letter to each square, to form four ordinary words.

TOYBO

KUYDS

GOAUNT

ZIRDAL

WHAT DID ONE
SKUNK SAY
TO THE OTHER?

Now arrange the circled letters to form the surprise answer, as suggested by the above cartoon.

Print answer here ⬜⬜ ⬜⬜ ⬜⬜⬜ !

JUMBLE ®

Unscramble these four Jumbles, one letter to
each square, to form four ordinary words.

GRUPE

BLAYM

DYRAMI

OTTYNK

WHAT COMES INTO
A HOUSE THROUGH
THE KEYHOLE?

Now arrange the circled letters to form
the surprise answer, as suggested by the
above cartoon.

Print answer here ◯ ◯◯◯

JUMBLE®

Unscramble these four Jumbles, one letter to each square, to form four ordinary words.

Psst!

WHAT THE
SECRETIVE
MUMMIES KEPT.

MYRIG

ATHEW

DASSIT

POWNEA

Now arrange the circled letters to form the surprise answer, as suggested by the above cartoon.

Print answer here ⬡⬡⬡⬡⬡⬡ UNDER ⬡⬡⬡⬡⬡

JUMBLE®

Unscramble these four Jumbles, one letter to
each square, to form four ordinary words.

LIXEE

YINCC

TIPIDE

BAAMEO

HELPS CONSTRUCTION
WORKERS TO STICK
TOGETHER.

Now arrange the circled letters to form
the surprise answer, as suggested by the
above cartoon.

Print answer here ⬡⬡⬡⬡⬡⬡

JUMBLE®

Unscramble these four Jumbles, one letter to each square, to form four ordinary words.

HINKT

ROLGY

ENDOTE

SABBOR

THE TEACHER HAD TO WEAR DARK GLASSES BECAUSE ALL THE KIDS WERE THIS.

Now arrange the circled letters to form the surprise answer, as suggested by the above cartoon.

Print answer here

JUMBLE®

Unscramble these four Jumbles, one letter to
each square, to form four ordinary words.

VOLEN

GHILT

EXVONC

LUDSON

WHAT SHE SENSED
VIOLETS MIGHT
"SIGNIFY."

Now arrange the circled letters to form
the surprise answer, as suggested by the
above cartoon.

Print answer here " ⬡⬡ ' ⬡ ⬡⬡⬡⬡⬡ "

JUMBLE®

Unscramble these four Jumbles, one letter to each square, to form four ordinary words.

LISEA

UNGED

LAWTUN

MORRAY

Doesn't surprise ME!

WHAT YOU MIGHT SAY WHEN YOU THINK OF A CHILD PRODIGY.

Now arrange the circled letters to form the surprise answer, as suggested by the above cartoon.

Print answer here

⬡⬡⬡⬡⬡ ⬡⬡⬡⬡⬡⬡ !

156

JUMBLE®

Unscramble these four Jumbles, one letter to each square, to form four ordinary words.

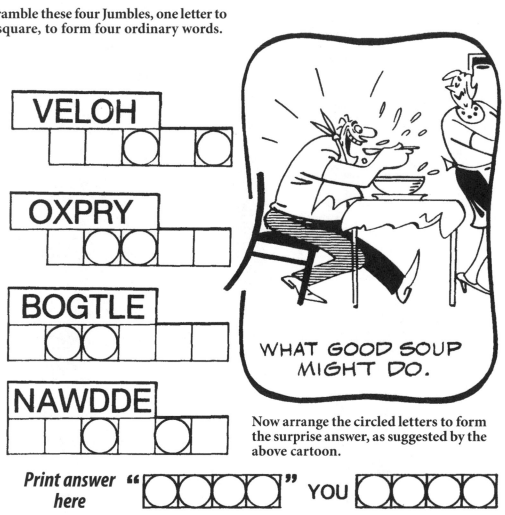

VELOH

OXPRY

BOGTLE

NAWDDE

WHAT GOOD SOUP MIGHT DO.

Now arrange the circled letters to form the surprise answer, as suggested by the above cartoon.

Print answer here "◯◯◯◯◯" YOU ◯◯◯◯

157

JUMBLE®

Unscramble these four Jumbles, one letter to
each square, to form four ordinary words.

SIFOT

TYLFO

LIFEED

PETICK

WHAT TWO WORDS
HAVE THE MOST
LETTERS IN THEM?

Now arrange the circled letters to form
the surprise answer, as suggested by the
above cartoon.

**Print answer
here**

158

JUMBLE®

Unscramble these four Jumbles, one letter to each square, to form four ordinary words.

DUELE

STUJO

BREEMM

REJUIN

WHAT YOU MIGHT SEE WHEN A BIG ELEPHANT SQUIRTS WATER FROM HIS TRUNK.

Now arrange the circled letters to form the surprise answer, as suggested by the above cartoon.

Print answer here A ⬡⬡⬡⬡⬡ ⬡⬡⬡

JUMBLE®

Unscramble these four Jumbles, one letter to
each square, to form four ordinary words.

KAYLE

MOECT

SMEECH

SPOOPE

WHAT **SLOT
MACHINES**
PRODUCE FOR
THEIR OWNERS.

Now arrange the circled letters to form
the surprise answer, as suggested by the
above cartoon.

Print
answer
here   " ☐☐☐☐ ☐☐☐☐ IN '☐☐' "

JUMBLE®

Unscramble these four Jumbles, one letter to
each square, to form four ordinary words.

USSOE

LUCCK

JUDSAT

INTOOL

Beautiful!

WHAT ARE YOUR
EYES FOR?

Now arrange the circled letters to form
the surprise answer, as suggested by the
above cartoon.

Print answer here ⬭⬭⬭⬭ FOR ⬭⬭⬭⬭⬭⬭

JUMBLE®

Unscramble these four Jumbles, one letter to each square, to form four ordinary words.

VEYHA
◯ ◯ ☐ ◯

RITHM
◯ ◯ ☐ ◯

HYNTAS
◯ ☐ ◯ ☐ ☐ ☐

MORNED
◯ ☐ ◯ ☐ ☐ ☐

WHAT HAPPENED TO LADY GODIVA'S HORSE WHEN HE SAW SHE HAD NO CLOTHES ON?

Now arrange the circled letters to form the surprise answer, as suggested by the above cartoon.

Print answer here IT ☐☐☐☐☐ ☐☐☐ "☐☐☐"

Lunar JUMBLE®

Challenger Puzzles

JUMBLE®

Unscramble these six Jumbles, one letter to each square, to form six ordinary words.

DUPLED

CLUBEK

TINISS

REUMED

EECCAD

INGOPE

WHAT DAVID DID TO GOLIATH.

Now arrange the circled letters to form the surprise answer, as suggested by the above cartoon.

Print answer here

" ⬡⬡⬡⬡⬡⬡ " HIM TO ⬡⬡⬡⬡⬡

JUMBLE®

Unscramble these six Jumbles, one letter to
each square, to form six ordinary words.

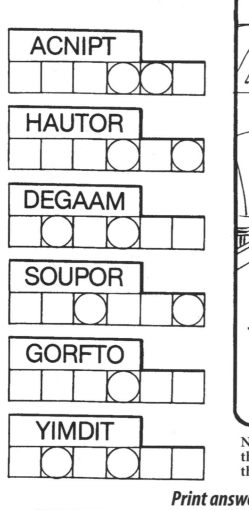

ACNIPT

HAUTOR

DEGAAM

SOUPOR

GORFTO

YIMDIT

THE KIND OF STORY
THAT WOULDN'T
INTEREST THIS GUY
AT ALL.

Now arrange the circled letters to form
the surprise answer, as suggested by
the above cartoon.

Print answer here

A ◯◯◯◯◯ – ◯◯◯◯◯◯◯◯ ONE

JUMBLE®

Unscramble these six Jumbles, one letter to
each square, to form six ordinary words.

NIMEUM

LISHEC

CODJUN

SABDUR

DOUSEX

PEBICS

HOW THOSE SINGERS
COMMUNICATED.

Now arrange the circled letters to form
the surprise answer, as suggested by
the above cartoon.

Print answer here

THEY "⬡⬡⬡⬡⬡⬡ – ⬡⬡⬡⬡⬡⬡"

JUMBLE®

Unscramble these six Jumbles, one letter to
each square, to form six ordinary words.

FELGUN

BERICK

YUNCAL

NAHRGE

DACUDE

CURSIC

WHAT THAT PHONY
BRAIN SURGEON
PRACTICED.

Now arrange the circled letters to form
the surprise answer, as suggested by
the above cartoon.

Print answer here

" ◯◯◯◯◯◯   ◯◯◯◯◯◯◯◯ "

167

JUMBLE®

Unscramble these six Jumbles, one letter to
each square, to form six ordinary words.

REBOFE

ASHIMP

BAUSCA

CHUGAT

FUNMIF

WEVILS

WHAT YOU
SAW WHEN THOSE
NEW NEXT-DOOR
NEIGHBORS GAVE THEIR
FIRST BIG PARTY.

Now arrange the circled letters to form
the surprise answer, as suggested by
the above cartoon.

Print answer here

THE ⬡⬡⬡⬡⬡ ⬡⬡⬡⬡⬡⬡⬡⬡⬡

JUMBLE®

Unscramble these six Jumbles, one letter to each square, to form six ordinary words.

TANGOU

BUNGIL

LAIFAC

GOIBLE

OURSEA

LAGYAX

We've been everywhere

WHAT THOSE PRETENTIOUS TRAVELERS RETURNED WITH PLENTY OF.

Now arrange the circled letters to form the surprise answer, as suggested by the above cartoon.

Print answer here

" ⬡⬡⬡⬡⬡ & ⬡⬡⬡⬡⬡⬡⬡⬡ "

JUMBLE®

Unscramble these six Jumbles, one letter to
each square, to form six ordinary words.

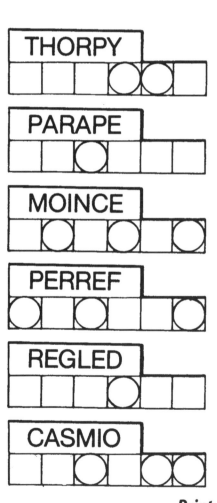

THORPY

PARAPE

MOINCE

PERREF

REGLED

CASMIO

WHERE THE
LUMBERJACK WENT
BEFORE CHRISTMAS.

Now arrange the circled letters to form
the surprise answer, as suggested by
the above cartoon.

Print answer here

ON A " ⬚⬚⬚⬚⬚⬚⬚⬚⬚⬚ " ⬚⬚⬚⬚⬚⬚

JUMBLE®

Unscramble these six Jumbles, one letter to each square, to form six ordinary words.

TAYFUL

MARKEB

LEHBED

ROQUIL

GOLFAN

SEDGIT

WHAT THE SUCCESSFUL REALTOR HAD.

Now arrange the circled letters to form the surprise answer, as suggested by the above cartoon.

Print answer here

" ◯◯◯◯ " TO BE ◯◯◯◯◯◯◯◯◯◯ FOR

JUMBLE®

Unscramble these six Jumbles, one letter to each square, to form six ordinary words.

MARFFI

NOMMOC

UNMEBB

BRUCHE

FLOSSI

GINDHI

A very lonely man

WHAT THE MISER KEPT.

Now arrange the circled letters to form the surprise answer, as suggested by the above cartoon.

Print answer here

TOO ⬡⬡⬡⬡ TO ⬡⬡⬡⬡⬡⬡⬡⬡

JUMBLE®

Unscramble these six Jumbles, one letter to each square, to form six ordinary words.

STIFIM

TEEBEL

PRAMCE

TASHAG

RIPIAM

HERDIT

If I say so myself, I'm terrific!

WHAT THAT EGOTISTICAL DOCTOR WAS.

Now arrange the circled letters to form the surprise answer, as suggested by the above cartoon.

Print answer here

AN " ☐ " ☐☐☐☐☐☐☐☐☐☐☐☐☐

JUMBLE®

Unscramble these six Jumbles, one letter to
each square, to form six ordinary words.

WHAYNO

MESECH

ROGDEC

YINCLE

BOICED

FLATES

IS THAT "SPOOK"
WHO'S RUNNING
FOR OFFICE LIKELY
TO GET ELECTED?

Now arrange the circled letters to form
the surprise answer, as suggested by
the above cartoon.

Print answer here

NOT
A ⬡⬡⬡⬡⬡ OF
A ⬡⬡⬡⬡⬡⬡⬡

JUMBLE®

Unscramble these six Jumbles, one letter to each square, to form six ordinary words.

RIGDIF

NUIJER

TENGLE

WADROC

RENOSP

TURBLE

PRIVATE

WHAT THAT OVERLY PROTECTIVE OFFICE RECEPTIONIST WAS.

Now arrange the circled letters to form the surprise answer, as suggested by the above cartoon.

Print answer here

A ⬡⬡⬡⬡⬡⬡⬡⬡⬡⬡⬡⬡⬡⬡⬡

JUMBLE®

Unscramble these six Jumbles, one letter to each square, to form six ordinary words.

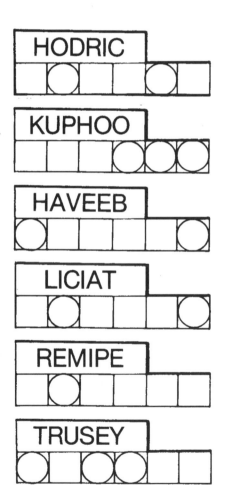

HODRIC

KUPHOO

HAVEEB

LICIAT

REMIPE

TRUSEY

WHAT A TAILGATER IS.

Now arrange the circled letters to form the surprise answer, as suggested by the above cartoon.

Print answer here

A ☐☐☐☐☐☐☐ ☐☐☐☐☐☐☐☐

JUMBLE®

Unscramble these six Jumbles, one letter to
each square, to form six ordinary words.

VINNET

HONUKO

GAYCEN

SMIHOD

MARLOF

LAPPOR

WHAT MANY A
VETERAN PRIZE
FIGHTER HAS BEEN.

Now arrange the circled letters to form
the surprise answer, as suggested by
the above cartoon.

Print answer here

⬡⬡⬡⬡⬡⬡⬡ THE ⬡⬡⬡⬡⬡

JUMBLE®

Unscramble these six Jumbles, one letter to each square, to form six ordinary words.

At least THIS is relaxing!

REDONP

STYLUB

PANOWE

ASTUNE

KORREB

BUTSOE

WHAT A MAN MIGHT TRY TO DO ON THE GOLF COURSE.

Now arrange the circled letters to form the surprise answer, as suggested by the above cartoon.

Print answer here

" ☐☐☐☐ " AWAY HIS ☐☐☐☐☐☐☐☐☐

JUMBLE®

Unscramble these six Jumbles, one letter to
each square, to form six ordinary words.

INTYME

HETTER

NOVCOY

DREBIG

FONLEY

LIVRIE

Here—take it all! I don't
want to get into any kind of
trouble with the law!

IRS

A SMART INCOME
TAX PAYER
KNOWS THAT IT'S
BETTER TO DO THIS.

Now arrange the circled letters to form
the surprise answer, as suggested by
the above cartoon.

Print answer here

⬡⬡⬡⬡⬡ THAN ⬡⬡⬡⬡⬡⬡⬡

JUMBLE®

Unscramble these six Jumbles, one letter to
each square, to form six ordinary words.

GIMINT

HUCNAH

PRYNTA

YOGAVE

CALDIP

CONTOY

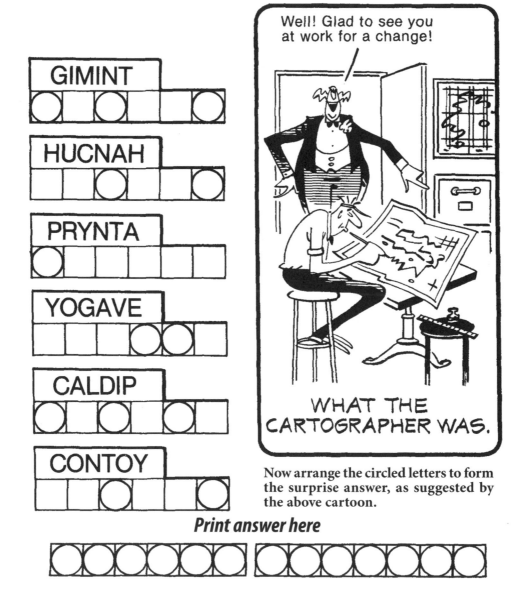

Well! Glad to see you
at work for a change!

**WHAT THE
CARTOGRAPHER WAS.**

Now arrange the circled letters to form
the surprise answer, as suggested by
the above cartoon.

Print answer here

JUMBLE®

Unscramble these six Jumbles, one letter to
each square, to form six ordinary words.

ENPOTT

NAYYAW

ELLGAY

DETHOB

INFEED

NAMORT

How
about
next
Tuesday?

How about
next month?

Next
year?

Sorry, all
booked up

WHAT KIND OF AN
EXISTENCE DID THAT
POPULAR GIRL LEAD?

Now arrange the circled letters to form
the surprise answer, as suggested by
the above cartoon.

Print answer here

A " ⬡⬡⬡⬡⬡ – ⬡⬡ – ⬡⬡⬡⬡ " ONE

JUMBLE®

Unscramble these six Jumbles, one letter to each square, to form six ordinary words.

RECRON
⬜◯⬜⬜◯⬜⬜

KLARET
⬜◯◯⬜⬜⬜

YONTUB
⬜⬜◯⬜⬜◯⬜

TUMPIE
◯⬜◯◯⬜⬜

UNCHAP
⬜◯⬜⬜⬜⬜

KUPPEE
⬜⬜⬜◯⬜◯

AN USHERETTE
SHOULD KNOW
HOW TO DO THIS.

Now arrange the circled letters to form the surprise answer, as suggested by the above cartoon.

Print answer here

◯◯◯ A ◯◯◯ IN HIS ◯◯◯◯◯

JUMBLE®

Unscramble these six Jumbles, one letter to
each square, to form six ordinary words.

RAUFIN

SWOBET

YERTAW

IPCINC

GANFIC

DITNIC

PROCESSING
PLANT

Shh—don't
disturb
him

HOW THE
ORANGE JUICE
PRODUCER BECAME
SO SUCCESSFUL.

Now arrange the circled letters to form
the surprise answer, as suggested by
the above cartoon.

Print answer here

BY " ◯◯◯◯◯◯◯◯◯◯◯◯◯◯◯◯◯ "

Answers

1. **Jumbles:** PUTTY CANAL DEPICT THORAX
Answer: What the manicurist's customer was getting —
OUT OF HAND

2. **Jumbles:** NOISY EJECT RANCID AROUND
Answer: What the loafer who was born with a silver spoon in
his mouth hasn't done since — STIRRED

3. **Jumbles:** GROIN SNARL ASSURE EULOGY
Answer: This should only be done with good taste —
SEASONING

4. **Jumbles:** MESSY HEFTY EIGHT DAMPEN
Answer: You might see eye to eye with someone who's this
— THE SAME HEIGHT

5. **Jumbles:** FRUIT EXPERT DROWSY SPRUCE
Answer: Instead of ice cream, epicures might "go for" this —
"PURE ICES"

6. **Jumbles:** HAIRY CHANT SHADOW LIMBER
Answer: Something you're sure to find in an algebra
instructor, if he's as smart as he should be — "BRAINS"

7. **Jumbles:** LUSTY KNIFE POISON TRUANT
Answer: He might seem hospitable, but not to be trusted
when he does this — "TAKES YOU IN"

8. **Jumbles:** THICK DALLY HELIUM CANNED
Answer: "Aimed" to provide channels for communication —
"MEDIA"

9. **Jumbles:** CARGO LOGIC GOLFER THRIVE
Answer: What the passengers got when the air conditioning
failed — HOT UNDER THE COLLAR

10. **Jumbles:** GULCH SCARF PEWTER KERNEL
Answer: By a stroke of luck, this fish got away — or so it
sounds — A "FLUKE"

11. **Jumbles:** BROOD FAINT EASILY LEDGER
Answer: She's a temptingly beautiful woman — and might
deliver a warning — A SIREN

12. **Jumbles:** WAGON BROOK GUTTER CORNEA
Answer: To make this, the farmer wore a shoe that was too
tight — HIS CORN GROW

13. **Jumbles:** PUPPY FLUID HEIFER PERSON
Answer: What he saw from the Eiffel Tower — AN "EYEFUL"

14. **Jumbles:** VALET YACHT SAVORY CHISEL
Answer: What they called that actor who always played the
villain — THE HEAVY "HEAVY"

15. **Jumbles:** LYRIC STUNG INFANT UNFAIR
Answer: What the orchard owner's life proved to be —
VERY FRUITFUL

16. **Jumbles:** PRINT SILKY DEADLY POROUS
Answer: One of two ways to breathe — A NOSTRIL

17. **Jumbles:** UNIFY CRAZE FEWEST TOWARD
Answer: It seems rather funny that all five vowels appear in
this word in their correct order — "FACETIOUS"

18. **Jumbles:** JOLLY CHAFF DECODE PESTLE
Answer: What the guy who hid his wallet in the freezer was
left with — COLD CASH

19. **Jumbles:** SKULK GULLY JOBBER SAVAGE
Answer: What those ants at the picnic do — "BUG" US

20. **Jumbles:** SWASH GUMMY AERATE FINITE
Answer: When the fog clears up, it won't be this — "MIST"

21. **Jumbles:** TITLE ESSAY DECENT MEMOIR
Answer: What a successful bachelor does, whichever way
you look at it — "MEETS ESTEEM"

22. **Jumbles:** NIECE TRULY GRAVEN WEDGED
Answer: What the swimming pool contractor did when
business fell off — WENT UNDER

23. **Jumbles:** HURRY GIVEN JAGGED ALPACA
Answer: What many expenses connected with the dairy
business might be — "IN CURD"

24. **Jumbles:** HAVOC PAUSE CEMENT FACILE
Answer: They enjoyed that vacation in the South Pacific
so much that they decided to go back for this — "SAMOA"
(some more)

25. **Jumbles:** EVENT AWOKE SOIREE FEWEST
Answer: When he went on that 14-day diet, this was all he
lost — TWO WEEKS

26. **Jumbles:** JEWEL HEFTY HITHER UNSEAT
Answer: It's good manners to try to make your guests feel at
home, especially when you wish this — THEY WERE

27. **Jumbles:** FORUM BISON ITALIC HAWKER
Answer: He fiddles while his listeners do this —
A SLOW BURN

28. **Jumbles:** INLET DOUSE LACING IGUANA
Answer: When his ship finally came in, he was too lazy to do
this — UNLOAD IT

29. **Jumbles:** CRIME AISLE CACTUS KNOTTY
Answer: Could it be a raincoat for wear in the big town? —
A CITY SLICKER

30. **Jumbles:** EXILE VIRUS MUSCLE LEGACY
Answer: How far down was her bathing suit cut? —
TO "SEE" LEVEL

31. **Jumbles:** FETCH TRAIT EXPEND TURKEY
Answer: What he and his girl were — PRETTY THICK

32. **Jumbles:** DROOP WHILE MUSLIN TOWARD
Answer: Why the business tycoon rushed off on a much
needed vacation — TO SLOW DOWN

33. **Jumbles:** FUDGE GUESS THWART OBLIGE
Answer: What some work in the garden can leave one —
"BUSHED"

34. **Jumbles:** THINK FENCE GIMLET CRAVAT
Answer: Don't expect someone to talk turkey who's this —
CHICKEN

35. **Jumbles:** PIECE WEARY HECKLE CASKET
Answer: What they called the eccentric cabdriver —
A WACKY HACKIE

36. **Jumbles:** ABIDE FUSSY CENSUS GLOBAL
Answer: What the boss was "breaking into" — "SOBS"

37. **Jumbles:** BUMPY FAULT CHISEL LOCALE
Answer: How the waitress acted when she spilled the gravy
— SAUCY

38. **Jumbles:** VIGIL NEWLY CATNIP BANANA
Answer: What the archer was — "BENT" ON WINNING

39. **Jumbles:** WHOSE PAGAN RUBBER BESTOW
Answer: Such fruit is not considered much good when
unobtainable — SOUR GRAPES

40. **Jumbles:** FIFTY BOOTY LIMPID BEFORE
Answer: Such a warning sounds "pointless" — A TIP-OFF

41. **Jumbles:** PLUSH DOWNY INDICT FOSSIL
Answer: Could be all that fighter ever licked — HIS WOUNDS

42. **Jumbles:** PRINT FUZZY OUTLET COMEDY
Answer: Could it be a sound from a dog without a pedigree?
— A "MUTT-ER"

43. **Jumbles:** DOILY GUIDE MINGLE SADIST
Answer: What the absentminded hen did —
MISLAID AN EGG

44. **Jumbles:** MAIZE SOAPY UNSOLD CAMPUS
Answer: Music that might accompany a turkey dinner —
A "YAM" SESSION

45. **Jumbles:** OCCUR KHAKI BROKEN POROUS
Answer: How does that fisherman who tends sheep on the side making a living? — BY HOOK OR BY CROOK

46. **Jumbles:** ELOPE ROBOT STYLUS FECUND
Answer: What life was for the unlucky gardener —
NO BED OF ROSES

47. **Jumbles:** LILAC PAUSE JESTER KINGLY
Answer: How she felt when she arrived home after a shopping binge — ALL "SPENT"

48. **Jumbles:** FORGO TEMPO CRAVAT LICHEN
Answer: What kind of plans was the architect making for him? — TO GET HOME

49. **Jumbles:** BATON GLAND CRAYON HALVED
Answer: What no upright person would do — LEAN

50. **Jumbles:** PRIOR MAUVE FORGET DULCET
Answer: Words you might get from Voltaire — "I LOVE ART"

51. **Jumbles:** SUEDE GUESS CANOPY PALLID
Answer: Did hangmen carry out such sentences? —
SUSPENDED ONES

52. **Jumbles:** OUTDO PIOUS COUPON MISUSE
Answer: What a ladle is — A SOUP SCOOP

53. **Jumbles:** POUND FELON BALLET HOOKUP
Answer: The skeleton was burning the midnight oil because he wanted to do this — BONE UP

54. **Jumbles:** LINER MINUS CHARGE PENMAN
Answer: Metal devices that help keep locks in place —
HAIRPINS

55. **Jumbles:** AMUSE TITLE JINGLE BIGAMY
Answer: What a girl sometimes wears at the beach —
A BAITING SUIT

56. **Jumbles:** YOUTH FORUM MISFIT ACCENT
Answer: A job for someone who's well-padded — "CUSHY"

57. **Jumbles:** RAVEN VITAL EMERGE BICEPS
Answer: A fruitful source of information — THE GRAPEVINE

58. **Jumbles:** PRONE VALVE FOURTH CAUCUS
Answer: How they clapped their hands when she sang —
OVER THEIR EARS

59. **Jumbles:** PRIZE LATCH OUTLET HARBOR
Answer: What she hoped the bachelor would do about his way of life — "ALTAR" IT

60. **Jumbles:** EMBER PLAID NEGATE TANGLE
Answer: What he had to do every time she had an accident in the kitchen — EAT IT FOR DINNER

61. **Jumbles:** KNEEL LAUGH IMBIBE JOCKEY
Answer: They called him a colorful fighter because he was this most of the time — BLACK & BLUE

62. **Jumbles:** TRACT PHOTO ENMITY SUBURB
Answer: What a soap opera usually is — CORN ON THE SOB

63. **Jumbles:** DOILY ENSUE BEWARE COOKIE
Answer: What the pretty blond teacher was, as described by her pupils — BLUE-EYED

64. **Jumbles:** PARKA GRIEF CEMENT TRYING
Answer: What's the best age to get hitched? — "MARRI-AGE"

65. **Jumbles:** PIANO FEINT DEBATE BEDBUG
Answer: What a person who cheats on a diet is apt to do —
GAIN — IN THE END

66. **Jumbles:** ANNUL JUMBO UNPACK PYTHON
Answer: What an honest elevator man probably is —
ON THE UP & UP

67. **Jumbles:** BLESS DIRTY FIRING INDOOR
Answer: In this situation, you'll be very close to a fight —
RINGSIDE

68. **Jumbles:** DECAY HOIST ASTRAY BAKERY
Answer: Might be a current sensation — A SHOCK

69. **Jumbles:** UPPER NOBLE FASTEN TROPHY
Answer: How to stop someone from talking in the back of the car — PUT HER IN THE FRONT

70. **Jumbles:** BURST MILKY IMPOSE ABUSED
Answer: You can prove your uprightness by taking this line — PLUMB

71. **Jumbles:** PAPER CABLE FACING ISLAND
Answer: It's not completely a "collapse" — just this —
A "LAPSE"

72. **Jumbles:** GAUZE WALTZ NIMBLE GENIUS
Answer: You need to bide your time to play this —
THE WAITING GAME

73. **Jumbles:** EPOCH HAREM CASKET MOSQUE
Answer: Made an impression on the bridle path —
A HORSESHOE

74. **Jumbles:** DOWNY SORRY ELDEST PASTRY
Answer: What a dictionary nut is never likely to be —
AT A LOSS FOR WORDS

75. **Jumbles:** PLUME FABLE HOOKED LOCATE
Answer: Comes under pressure when a driver steps on it —
THE PEDAL

76. **Jumbles:** TWICE NOTCH RADISH SOOTHE
Answer: How far away did David stand from Goliath? —
A STONE'S THROW

77. **Jumbles:** TRULY BAGGY ANSWER BESTOW
Answer: How those artillerymen were going —
"GREAT GUNS"

78. **Jumbles:** ARRAY PIPER SECOND BUSHEL
Answer: What she said baking a good dessert was —
EASY AS PIE

79. **Jumbles:** TULIP CHALK OXYGEN QUIVER
Answer: How to dress on a very cold day — QUICKLY

80. **Jumbles:** CASTE MONEY ANYHOW BOILED
Answer: Why the cops couldn't catch up with the pickpocket — HE STOLE AWAY

81. **Jumbles:** REBEL GAVEL STUDIO RABBIT
Answer: What they said the dynamiters' annual shindig was — A REAL BLAST

82. **Jumbles:** GAUGE TACKY LIQUOR BEAVER
Answer: No, he was not after the family pet —
THE CAT BURGLAR

83. **Jumbles:** ELDER BRAWL QUORUM BUREAU
Answer: Could make one think of food — a line of men waiting for haircuts — A "BARBER QUEUE" (barbecue)

84. **Jumbles:** BROIL WHEEL ENCORE OMELET
Answer: What the newcomer made — "MEN COWER"

85. **Jumbles:** COUGH GIANT INLAID MINGLE
Answer: This is the key to all good driving — IGNITION

86. **Jumbles:** AWARD OUNCE GOPHER INBORN
Answer: Might provide some rest for a tired fish —
THE OCEAN BED

87. **Jumbles:** WOMEN JUICE ALWAYS BICKER
Answer: What those hoboes were telling — "BUM" JOKES

88. **Jumbles:** BANJO CYCLE THRASH DECEIT
Answer: What the man who invented the slide fastener hoped it would do — "CATCH ON"

89. **Jumbles:** NIECE LIBEL BROGUE HEARTH
Answer: Not the whole story of Lady Godiva — just this —
A "BARE" OUTLINE

90. **Jumbles:** CROWN QUEST ADRIFT FLURRY
Answer: What tune makes a performer happy? — A "FOR-TUNE"

91. **Jumbles:** MERCY FEVER ZEALOT GAMBLE
Answer: What sailing a boat might be for an experience sailor — A "BREEZE"

92. **Jumbles:** PHONY RUMMY AUTUMN FALLEN
Answer: On which he placed money of a certain amount — A MOUNT

93. **Jumbles:** LIMBO MADAM BLUISH MAGPIE
Answer: Where it could be said at a banquet — THE "DAIS"

94. **Jumbles:** QUEER BARGE INJURY FORCED
Answer: What the heavy smoker was advised to do — REDUCE

95. **Jumbles:** WAFER RAINY STURDY CROTCH
Answer: Due for a "roasting" from the seargeant — A "RAW" RECRUIT

96. **Jumbles:** FINAL AWOKE POSTAL BARREL
Answer: Could be the result of spinning a lot of tales — A WEB OF LIES

97. **Jumbles:** FLOUR ALTAR NIPPLE CANINE
Answer: For someone who plans to make a splash in the kitchen — AN APRON

98. **Jumbles:** BOWER FLANK GATHER FIDDLE
Answer: Still a student — but he has within him the ability to make money — A "L-EARNER'

99. **Jumbles:** LADLE FUSSY DEPUTY CUDGEL
Answer: How he looked after spending the whole day planting the garden — "SEEDY"

100. **Jumbles:** PIETY MOUTH NEWEST STRONG
Answer: It's set to leave you in the dark — THE SUN (the sunset)

101. **Jumbles:** LYING ERASE BRIDLE CUDDLE
Answer: Obviously not a fly-by-night — THE EARLY BIRD

102. **Jumbles:** PATIO STEED CENSUS BLAZER
Answer: Suggested that he was proud of the fact that he worked less than anyone else — AN IDLE BOAST

103. **Jumbles:** HOUSE EATEN GARISH ACHING
Answer: What one mouse said to the other as he saw the trap being baited — "CHEESE IT"

104. **Jumbles:** NAÏVE AROMA PANTRY GARLIC
Answer: An article of clothing a gentleman might have around the arm — "G-ARM-ENT"

105. **Jumbles:** AFTER PIKER JOYFUL MALLET
Answer: What the gambler named his daughter — KITTY

106. **Jumbles:** MOLDY ORBIT HARDLY MEASLY
Answer: Ran off with a roll of cloth — "BOLT-ED"

107. **Jumbles:** CHESS FOYER TUMULT JUMPER
Answer: To know this was the very apex of the spy's ambition — TOP SECRET

108. **Jumbles:** BULLY LOWLY AFRAID ELEVEN
Answer: The sort of life you might expect a glutton to lead — A FULL ONE

109. **Jumbles:** CATCH DAILY ABRUPT MEDLEY
Answer: Where's the most difficult lock to pick? — ON A BALD HEAD

110. **Jumbles:** MUSTY PEONY ENGINE CRABBY
Answer: A title the boxer didn't aim to be out for — "COUNT"

111. **Jumbles:** POISE TUNED SCHOOL KILLER
Answer: When is a joke most effective? — WHEN IT STRIKES ONE

112. **Jumbles:** CRANK PLUSH EXCITE BOUNCE
Answer: The "disintegration" of one star may threaten the whole nation — "TREASON"

113. **Jumbles:** SLANT COCOA WIDEST HERMIT
Answer: Most duels are rather short affairs because they only require this — TWO SECONDS

114. **Jumbles:** FAVOR QUEEN AWHILE SATIRE
Answer: Not a bad thing to do when in court — SWEAR

115. **Jumbles:** GRIME HAVEN ARTFUL ENOUGH
Answer: What was the new bride's favorite fish? — "HER-RING"

116. **Jumbles:** CURIO FROZE ARCADE STOLEN
Answer: What he had on as a result of getting into a pickle — A SOUR FACE

117. **Jumbles:** SPURN POUCH MORTAR LAVISH
Answer: Could they be chiselers employed on "relief" projects? — SCULPTORS

118. **Jumbles:** ADAPT JEWEL BRUTAL MANIAC
Answer: There may be a fortune to be found at the bottom of this vessel — A TEACUP

119. **Jumbles:** BLOOD GLOAT PELVIS HAIRDO
Answer: The world's biggest hold-up man — ATLAS

120. **Jumbles:** SIEGE VIRUS TIPTOE DEBTOR
Answer: What some women claim to be — "DRESSTITUTE"

121. **Jumbles:** PERKY BISON UNEASY TACKLE
Answer: Looks at them coming and going — in both directions — SEES

122. **Jumbles:** DRAFT CHAMP PHYSIC ENTICE
Answer: What the "swell" guy had — A HEAD TO MATCH

123. **Jumbles:** EMERY RAPID POLISH COMPEL
Answer: How do you arrive at the top of a church steeple on a hot day? — "PER-SPIRE"

124. **Jumbles:** BORAX CAKED ABDUCT BUCKET
Answer: What gardening that begins at daybreak often ends up with — "BACKBREAK"

125. **Jumbles:** RUSTY POACH JAGUAR INDUCE
Answer: What people who cut you short on the phone evidently have — HANG-UPS

126. **Jumbles:** GLADE TRAIT MORGUE VACANT
Answer: A GREAT OVEN might produce most of this — "OVEREATING"

127. **Jumbles:** EVOKE BUSHY DECADE LIKELY
Answer: Vegetables that sound as though they should never be served aboard a ship — LEEKS

128. **Jumbles:** DAUNT CROON INFECT FAULTY
Answer: What some joggers tend to do — RUN TO FAT

129. **Jumbles:** GAILY FISHY KETTLE IMPAIR
Answer: When they got married, this could have been their "life's aim" — "FAMILIES"

130. **Jumbles:** ABOVE SNACK NUMBER INFUSE
Answer: Could be the result of everyone wanting to get into the act — A MOB SCENE

131. **Jumbles:** DIZZY QUIRE WAITER URCHIN
Answer: What a bright student is expected to do when there's an exam — WHIZ THROUGH THE QUIZ

132. **Jumbles:** GUILE ANNOY MORBID LAGOON
Answer: This material never gets worn out — LINING

133. **Jumbles:** BRIAR GOOSE AFFRAY DRUDGE
Answer: A big wheel in the amusement business — FERRIS

134. **Jumbles:** OWING WHILE POPLAR MUSCLE
Answer: The general's favorite headquarters — HIS PILLOW

135. **Jumbles:** GOING FLUKE BEFALL CORRAL
Answer: What vampires often take at midnight — A COFFIN BREAK

136. **Jumbles:** VENOM CURRY PAUPER FELONY
Answer: How to make varnish disappear — REMOVE THE R

137. **Jumbles:** IDIOT WEDGE TERROR SLOUCH
Answer: What that famous author became after he passed away — A "GHOST" WRITER

186

138. **Jumbles:** HENCE SKIMP DEFAME SEETHE
Answer: What a mermaid is — A DEEP SHE-FISH

139. **Jumbles:** NEWLY GNARL TIMELY SUBMIT
Answer: You might serve it to others, but you wouldn't want to eat it yourself — A TENNIS BALL

140. **Jumbles:** LOVER DITTO VERSUS MOHAIR
Answer: What a souped-up car that broke down was — A "SHOT" ROD

141. **Jumbles:** RIGOR BOUGH WEAKEN BLOODY
Answer: Why the bookworm visited the library — TO "BURROW" A BOOK

142. **Jumbles:** FETCH NATAL PICNIC INDUCT
Answer: Where you're apt to find the most fish — BETWEEN HEAD & TAIL

143. **Jumbles:** MINOR TWEET STIGMA CACTUS
Answer: An easy way to get on TV — SIT ON YOUR SET

144. **Jumbles:** DRYLY OBESE SWIVEL DRIVEL
Answer: What's a parrot? — A WORDY BIRDIE

145. **Jumbles:** TRIPE ROACH HYBRID TOTTER
Answer: What THE RADIATOR produced — "A TORRID HEAT"

146. **Jumbles:** COLIC STOKE BLUING PRISON
Answer: What the refrigerator did during the power failure — LOST ITS COOL

147. **Jumbles:** USURY LOUSY MAROON PLUNGE
Answer: Won first prize at the cat show — A GLAMOUR PUSS

148. **Jumbles:** BOOTY DUSKY NOUGAT LIZARD
Answer: What did one skunk say to the other? — SO DO YOU!

149. **Jumbles:** PURGE BALMY MYRIAD KNOTTY
Answer: What comes into the house through the keyhole? — A KEY

150. **Jumbles:** GRIMY WHEAT SADIST WEAPON
Answer: What the secretive mummies kept — THINGS UNDER WRAPS

151. **Jumbles:** EXILE CYNIC PITIED AMOEBA
Answer: Helps construction workers stick together — CEMENT

152. **Jumbles:** THINK GLORY DENOTE ABSORB
Answer: The teacher had to wear dark glasses because all the kids were this — SO BRIGHT

153. **Jumbles:** NOVEL LIGHT CONVEX UNSOLD
Answer: What she sensed violets might "signify" — "IT'S LOVE"

154. **Jumbles:** AISLE NUDGE WALNUT ARMORY
Answer: What you might say when you think of a child prodigy — SMALL WONDER!

155. **Jumbles:** HOVEL PROXY GOBLET DAWNED
Answer: What good soup might do — "BOWL" YOU OVER

156. **Jumbles:** FOIST LOFTY DEFILE PICKET
Answer: What two words have the most letters in them? — POST OFFICE

157. **Jumbles:** ELUDE JOUST MEMBER INJURE
Answer: What you might see when a big elephant squirts water from his trunk — A JUMBO JET

158. **Jumbles:** LEAKY COMET SCHEME OPPOSE
Answer: What SLOT MACHINES produce for their owners — "CASH LOST IN 'EM"

159. **Jumbles:** SOUSE CLUCK ADJUST LOTION
Answer: What are your eyes for? — JUST FOR LOOKS

160. **Jumbles:** HEAVY MIRTH SHANTY MODERN
Answer: What happened to Lady Godiva's horse when he saw she had no clothes on? — IT MADE HIM "SHY"

161. **Jumbles:** PUDDLE BUCKLE INSIST DEMURE ACCEDE PIGEON
Answer: What David did to Goliath — "ROCKED" HIM TO SLEEP

162. **Jumbles:** CATNIP AUTHOR DAMAGE POROUS FORGOT DIMITY
Answer: The kind of story that wouldn't interest this guy at all — A HAIR-RAISING ONE

163. **Jumbles:** IMMUNE CHISEL JOCUND ABSURD EXODUS BICEPS
Answer: How those singers communicated — THEY "CHORUS-PONDED"

164. **Jumbles:** ENGULF BICKER LUNACY HANGER ADDUCE CIRCUS
Answer: What that phony brain surgeon practiced — "SKULL DUGGERY"

165. **Jumbles:** BEFORE MISHAP ABACUS CAUGHT MUFFIN SWIVEL
Answer: What you saw when those new next-door neighbors gave their first big party — THE HOUSE SWARMING

166. **Jumbles:** NOUGAT BLUING FACIAL OBLIGE AROUSE GALAXY
Answer: What those pretentious travelers returned with plenty of — "BRAG & BAGGAGE"

167. **Jumbles:** TROPHY APPEAR INCOME PREFER LEDGER MOSAIC
Answer: Where the lumberjack went before Christmas — ON A "CHOPPING" SPREE

168. **Jumbles:** FAULTY EMBARK BEHELD LIQUOR FLAGON DIGEST
Answer: What the successful realtor had — " LOTS" TO BE THANKFUL FOR

169. **Jumbles:** AFFIRM COMMON BENUMB CHERUB FOSSIL HIDING
Answer: What the miser kept — TOO MUCH TO HIMSELF

170. **Jumbles:** MISFIT BEETLE CAMPER AGHAST IMPAIR DITHER
Answer: What that egotistical doctor was — AN "I" SPECIALIST

171. **Jumbles:** ANYHOW SCHEME CODGER NICELY BODICE FESTAL
Answer: Is that "spook" who's running for office likely to get elected? — NOT A GHOST OF A CHANCE

172. **Jumbles:** FRIGID INJURE GENTLE COWARD PERSON BUTLER
Answer: What that overly protective office receptionist was — A REJECTIONIST

173. **Jumbles:** ORCHID HOOKUP BEHAVE ITALIC EMPIRE SURETY
Answer: What a tailgater is — A BUMPER STICKER

174. **Jumbles:** INVENT UNHOOK AGENCY MODISH FORMAL POPLAR
Answer: What many a veteran prize fighter has been — THROUGH THE ROPES

175. **Jumbles:** PONDER SUBTLY WEAPON UNSEAT BROKER OBTUSE
Answer: What a man might try to do on the golf course — "PUTT" AWAY HIS TROUBLES

176. **Jumbles:** ENMITY TETHER CONVOY BRIDGE FELONY VIRILE
Answer: A smart income tax payer knows that it's better to do this — GIVE THAN DECEIVE

177. **Jumbles:** TIMING HAUNCH PANTRY VOYAGE PLACID TYCOON
Answer: What the cartographer was — CAUGHT MAPPING

178. **Jumbles:** POTENT ANYWAY GALLEY HOTBED DEFINE MATRON
Answer: What kind of existence did that popular girl lead? — A "DATE-TO-DATE" ONE

179. **Jumbles:** CORNER TALKER BOUNTY IMPUTE PAUNCH UPKEEP
Answer: An usherette should know how to do this — PUT A MAN IN HIS PLACE

180. **Jumbles:** UNFAIR BESTOW WATERY PICNIC FACING INDICT
Answer: How the orange juice producer became so successful — BY "CONCENTRATING"

187

Need More Jumbles®?

Jumble® Books

More than 175 puzzles each!

Jammin' Jumble®
$9.95 • ISBN: 1-57243-844-4

Java Jumble®
$9.95 • ISBN: 978-1-60078-415-6

Jazzy Jumble®
$9.95 • ISBN: 978-1-57243-962-7

Jet Set Jumble®
$9.95 • ISBN: 978-1-60078-353-1

Joyful Jumble®
$9.95 • ISBN: 978-1-60078-079-0

Juke Joint Jumble®
$9.95 • ISBN: 978-1-60078-295-4

Jumble® at Work
$9.95 • ISBN: 1-57243-147-4

Jumble® Celebration
$9.95 • ISBN: 978-1-60078-134-6

Jumble® Circus
$9.95 • ISBN: 978-1-60078-739-3

Jumble® Exploer
$9.95 • ISBN: 978-1-60078-854-3

Jumble® Explosion
$9.95 • ISBN: 978-1-60078-078-3

Jumble® Fever
$9.95 • ISBN: 1-57243-593-3

Jumble® Fiesta
$9.95 • ISBN: 1-57243-626-3

Jumble® Fun
$9.95 • ISBN: 1-57243-379-5

Jumble® Galaxy
$9.95 • ISBN: 978-1-60078-583-2

Jumble® Genius
$9.95 • ISBN: 1-57243-896-7

Jumble® Getaway
$9.95 • ISBN: 978-1-60078-547-4

Jumble® Grab Bag
$9.95 • ISBN: 1-57243-273-X

Jumble® Jackpot
$9.95 • ISBN: 1-57243-897-5

Jumble® Jambalaya
$9.95 • ISBN: 978-1-60078-294-7

Jumble® Jamboree
$9.95 • ISBN: 1-57243-696-4

Jumble® Jitterbug
$9.95 • ISBN: 978-1-60078-584-9

Jumble® Jubilee
$9.95 • ISBN: 1-57243-231-4

Jumble® Juggernaut
$9.95 • ISBN: 978-1-60078-026-4

Jumble® Junction
$9.95 • ISBN: 1-57243-380-9

Jumble® Jungle
$9.95 • ISBN: 978-1-57243-961-0

Jumble® Madness
$9.95 • ISBN: 1-892049-24-4

Jumble® Magic
$9.95 • ISBN: 978-1-60078-795-9

Jumble® Safari
$9.95 • ISBN: 978-1-60078-675-4

Jumble® See & Search
$9.95 • ISBN: 1-57243-549-6

Jumble® See & Search 2
$9.95 • ISBN: 1-57243-734-0

Jumble® Sensation
$9.95 • ISBN: 978-1-60078-548-1

Jumble® Surprise
$9.95 • ISBN: 1-57243-320-5

Jumble® Vacation
$9.95 • ISBN: 978-1-60078-796-6

Jumpin' Jumble®
$9.95 • ISBN: 978-1-60078-027-1

Lunar Jumble®
$9.95 • ISBN: 978-1-60078-853-6

Outer Space Jumble®
$9.95 • ISBN: 978-1-60078-416-3

Rainy Day Jumble®
$9.95 • ISBN: 978-1-60078-352-4

Ready, Set, Jumble®
$9.95 • ISBN: 978-1-60078-133-0

Rock 'n' Roll Jumble®
$9.95 • ISBN: 978-1-60078-674-7

Royal Jumble®
$9.95 • ISBN: 978-1-60078-738-6

Sports Jumble®
$9.95 • ISBN: 1-57243-113-X

Summer Fun Jumble®
$9.95 • ISBN: 1-57243-114-8

Travel Jumble®
$9.95 • ISBN: 1-57243-198-9

TV Jumble®
$9.95 • ISBN: 1-57243-461-9

Oversize Jumble® Books

More than 500 puzzles each!

Generous Jumble®
$19.95 • ISBN: 1-57243-385-X

Giant Jumble®
$19.95 • ISBN: 1-57243-349-3

Gigantic Jumble®
$19.95 • ISBN: 1-57243-426-0

Jumbo Jumble®
$19.95 • ISBN: 1-57243-314-0

The Very Best of Jumble® BrainBusters
$19.95 • ISBN: 1-57243-845-2

Jumble® Crosswords™

More than 175 puzzles each!

More Jumble® Crosswords™
$9.95 • ISBN: 1-57243-386-8

Jumble® Crosswords™ Jackpot
$9.95 • ISBN: 1-57243-615-8

Jumble® Crosswords™ Jamboree
$9.95 • ISBN: 1-57243-787-1

Jumble® BrainBusters™

More than 175 puzzles each!

Jumble® BrainBusters™
$9.95 • ISBN: 1-892049-28-7

Jumble® BrainBusters™ II
$9.95 • ISBN: 1-57243-424-4

Jumble® BrainBusters™ III
$9.95 • ISBN: 1-57243-463-5

Jumble® BrainBusters™ IV
$9.95 • ISBN: 1-57243-489-9

Jumble® BrainBusters™ 5
$9.95 • ISBN: 1-57243-548-8

Jumble® BrainBusters™ Bonanza
$9.95 • ISBN: 1-57243-616-6

Boggle™ BrainBusters™
$9.95 • ISBN: 1-57243-592-5

Boggle™ BrainBusters™ 2
$9.95 • ISBN: 1-57243-788-X

Jumble® BrainBusters™ Junior
$9.95 • ISBN: 1-892049-29-5

Jumble® BrainBusters™ Junior II
$9.95 • ISBN: 1-57243-425-2

Fun in the Sun with Jumble® BrainBusters™
$9.95 • ISBN: 1-57243-733-2